SWIMMING

Steps to Success

Second Edition

David G. Thomas, MS
Professor Emeritus
State University of New York—Binghamton

Human Kinetics

Library of Congress Cataloging-in-Publication Data

Thomas, David G., 1924-
    Swimming : steps to success / David G. Thomas. — 2nd ed.
        p.   cm. -- (Steps to success activity series)
    ISBN 0-87322-846-4
    1. Swimming.   I. Title.   II. Series.
    GV837.T47   1996
    797.2'1--dc20

                                                                                                    95-42642
                                                                                                    CIP

ISBN: 0-87322-846-4

Series and Developmental Editor: Judy Patterson Wright, PhD; **Assistant Editor:** John Wentworth; **Editorial Assistant:** Jennifer Hemphill; **Copyeditor:** June Waldman; **Proofreader:** Sue Fetters; **Typesetter:** Kathy Boudreau-Fuoss; **Text Designer:** Keith Blomberg; **Layout Artist:** Denise Lowry; **Cover Designer:** Jack Davis; **Photographer (cover):** Wilmer Zehr; **Illustrators:** Bonnie Hammer and Keith Blomberg; **Printer:** United Graphics

Instructional Designer for the Steps to Success Activity Series: Joan N. Vickers, EdD, University of Calgary, Calgary, Alberta, Canada

Human Kinetics books are available at special discounts for bulk purchase. Special editions or book excerpts can also be created to specification. For details, contact the Special Sales Manager at Human Kinetics.

Printed in the United States of America   10   9   8   7   6   5   4

Human Kinetics
Web site: http://www.humankinetics.com/

United States: Human Kinetics, P.O. Box 5076, Champaign, IL 61825-5076
1-800-747-4457
e-mail: humank@hkusa.com

Canada: Human Kinetics, 475 Devonshire Road, Unit 100, Windsor, ON N8Y 2L5
1-800-465-7301 (in Canada only)
e-mail: humank@hkcanada.com

Europe: Human Kinetics, P.O. Box IW14, Leeds LS16 6TR, United Kingdom
+44 (0)113-278 1708
e-mail: humank@hkeurope.com

Australia: Human Kinetics, 57A Price Avenue, Lower Mitcham, South Australia 5062
(08) 82771555
e-mail: humank@hkaustralia.com

New Zealand: Human Kinetics, P.O. Box 105-231, Auckland Central
09-523-3462
e-mail: humank@hknewz.com

CONTENTS

PREFACE

Swimming—"You can't find a better sport to save your life." So said Commodore Wilbert E. Longfellow, founder of the American Red Cross swimming program. How true his statement is, but it touches only one aspect of a sport that has much more to offer. Great satisfaction results from feeling at home in the water. Swimming is a wholesome, confidence-building activity; it is both relaxing and invigorating.

This second edition of *Swimming: Steps to Success* is unique in that it focuses on the inherent buoyancy of the human body as a basis for all swimming strokes. Even such accomplished swimmers as Olympic stars Betsy Mitchell and Tom Jager started their careers with simple front and back floats. They added a few arm and leg motions and went on to win Olympic medals!

Almost everyone—95% of all men and 99% of all women—can float motionless while holding a deep breath. Those who cannot float motionless can achieve the floating position with minor movements of the arms or legs. Swimming is so easy; it takes less effort than almost any other sport.

In this second edition the sequence of steps has been altered to enhance logical progression, and some steps have been combined to shorten the learning process. Teaching aids are introduced earlier in the second edition to ease the transition to a liquid environment.

Following the instructions in this book will lead you to a new and fascinating activity. CAUTION—Swimming may be habit forming! It may change your life and may even make *you* a national champion!

We present here a sequence of steps that will get you moving through the water in the quickest way possible. No other beginner swimming book introduces you to the mask and snorkel before you start a prone float. Yet, the mask and snorkel make prone swimming so much easier that it makes good sense to use them early. Once you realize that your body is buoyant, you will immediately begin to use recognized stroke patterns for four of the best known swimming strokes.

Sequential drills take you through the preliminary movement patterns and directly into the strokes. Follow the steps and drills carefully as they build, one upon the other, for the quickest route to success.

In writing this book I must recognize the many hundreds of my students who taught me all I know about swimming and the remarkable editing skills of Dr. Judy Patterson Wright of the Human Kinetics staff.

THE STEPS TO SUCCESS STAIRCASE

Get ready to climb a staircase—one that will lead you to be a great swimmer. You cannot leap to the top; you get there by climbing one step at a time.

Each of the 12 steps you will take is an easy transition from the one before. The first few steps of the staircase provide a foundation—a solid foundation of basic skills and concepts. As you progress further, you will learn how to connect groups of these seemingly isolated skills. Practicing common combinations of swimming skills will give you the experience you need to begin making natural and accurate decisions in the water. You will learn to choose the proper stroke to match your various swimming needs—whether speed, ease, distance, or fun. As you near the top of the staircase, the climb will ease, and you'll find that you have developed a sense of confidence in your swimming ability that makes further progress a real joy.

To prepare to become a good climber, familiarize yourself with this section, as well as the "Swimming Today" section for orientation and in order to understand how to set up your practice sessions around the steps.

Follow the same sequence each step of the way;

1. Read the explanation of what is covered in each step, why the step is important, and how to execute or perform the step's focus, which may be on basic skills or concepts, or on a combination of the two.
2. Follow the numbered illustrations showing exactly how to position your body to execute each basic skill successfully. There are two or three general parts to each skill that show the progression from the preparation (getting into a starting position), to the execution (performing the skill that is the focus of the step), and sometimes, to the follow-through (recovering to starting position).
3. Look over the common Success Stoppers that may occur and the recommendations for how to correct them.
4. Read the directions for each drill, think about the Success Checks as you perform the drill, and practice until you can attain the Success Goal listed for that drill. If the drill seems too easy or too difficult, use the suggestions under each drill to increase or decrease the difficulty to fit your skill level. Meet the Success Goal for each drill before moving on to the next one, because the drills are arranged in an easy-to-difficult progression. This sequence is designed specifically to help you achieve continual success. The drills help you improve through repetition and purposeful practice.
5. As soon as you can reach all the Success Goals in one step, you are ready for a qualified observer—such as a swimming instructor or a skilled swimmer friend—to evaluate your basic skill technique against the Keys to Success for each skill. This is a qualitative or subjective evaluation of your basic technique or form, because using correct form can enhance your performance. Your evaluator may be able to tailor some specific drills to improve your skills.

6. Repeat these procedures for each of the 12 Steps to Success. Then rate yourself according to the directions in the Rating Your Progress section.

Good luck on your step-by-step journey to developing your swimming skills, building confidence, experiencing success, and having fun!

SWIMMING TODAY

In ancient times people took to the water to avoid a forest fire, to escape an enemy, to search for food, or simply to find relief from the blazing sun. Whatever the reason, the history of swimming through the ages is fascinating. Women and men are drawn to the water by an unexplainable force. Children seek puddles to play in. Sailors march irresistibly to the sea. Vacationers flock to the seaside for the soothing sights and sounds of the water.

For some, like Olympic swimmers Janet Evans and Tracy Caulkins, water is a medium of challenge. They met the challenge through intense practice and fierce competition on the international level, and they achieved victory and honor for their country. Rowdy Gaines and Matt Biondi know all about being at home in the water. From the day they started training for a place on the U.S. Olympic team, these Olympic stars have spent a significant portion of their lives in the water. Aquatic challenge and competition have been major forces in their lives and have led them to the pinnacle of success, fame, and fortune.

You, too, can experience the mysterious forces of the aquatic environment by learning to swim. Swimming provides amusement, relaxation, challenge, competition, and the ability to save your life in an aquatic emergency.

The first phase of accomplishment in the water is learning to swim. If you follow the natural laws of buoyancy and propulsion, you can swim easily in any position, expending as much or as little energy as you wish, at any age from 1 to 91.

Swimming does not require a set pattern of arm or leg movements. You may use any arm and leg movements that allow you to remain at the surface and move from one place to another. Certain combinations of motions, however, are more efficient than others. Swimmers package these efficient motions into recognized *strokes*. The best known swimming strokes are the sidestroke, the crawl stroke, the elementary backstroke, the breaststroke, the back crawl, and the butterfly stroke. We teach the first four of these strokes in this book. The others are explored in *Advanced Swimming: Steps to Success*.

The sidestroke is the most powerful of all the strokes. Because of its power, lifesavers use the sidestroke to rescue drowning victims. The crawl stroke is the fastest and most efficient stroke. The elementary backstroke is the easiest and safest stroke for conservation of energy, and the breaststroke is a restful stroke that allows you to keep your head above water, to see where you are going, and even to converse with your swimming buddy.

The field of water safety is a growing field that offers challenges to anyone who wishes to make a career of aquatics. Leadership positions in lifeguarding, swim instruction, and swim facility operation and management are constantly expanding as aquatic sports gain in popularity.

If your interest lies in swim instruction or lifesaving and lifeguarding, you will want to be familiar with the programs of the American Red Cross and the Young Men's Christian

Association (YMCA). If competition is your forte, you may want to become involved in speed swimming through a national organization such as U.S. Swimming Inc. Other areas of aquatic competition and their sponsoring organizations are water polo (U.S. Water Polo); synchronized swimming (U.S. Syncho Inc.); underwater hockey (National Underwater Hockey Assoc.); springboard diving (U.S. Diving Inc.); competitive lifesaving (National Surf Lifesaving Assoc.); fin swimming (Underwater Society of America); and scuba diving (National Association of Underwater Instructors, Professional Association of Diving Instructors, and others). The basis for all aquatic competition, however, is right here in this book. The skills we teach here are the beginning point for the whole fascinating world of aquatics.

The dangers inherent in entering the water are such that all aquatic participants must observe certain rules of personal safety and conduct. Some of the most important rules follow.

Never swim alone. Always have someone with you who can either help or get help in an emergency.

Know the area where you plan to swim. Know the locations of the deep and shallow water and find out about any hidden hazards that are not apparent from above the water.

Never swim immediately after eating. Wait at least 30 minutes after a light meal and longer after a heavy meal.

Never chew gum while swimming. Breathing patterns in swimming require a clear mouth and throat.

Do not run, push, or indulge in horseplay on a pool deck. The area is usually wet and slippery, and accidents can happen easily.

You'll use the following items of equipment as you follow the drills in this book:

Kickboard
Leg float (sometimes called a "pull buoy")
Face mask
Pair of swim fins
Snorkel
"Deep-float" leg float
Float belt
Hula hoop
Though not required, you may prefer to wear goggles and a nose clip for many of the drills.
(See Figure 1.)

The first two items (kickboards and leg floats) are standard equipment items at most pools. You may be permitted to use them, or you can buy your own inexpensively. The next three items (face mask, swim fins, and snorkel) are personal-fit items. You'll want to supply your own for proper fit and for personal hygiene. Masks and fins are the most expensive items. Swim fins are not absolutely essential for completing the *steps to success* (chap-

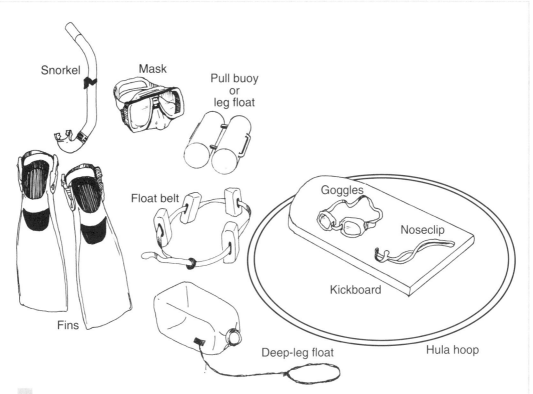

Figure 1   Equipment.

ters) in this book, but they are of considerable value. The next three items (deep-float leg float, float belt, and hula hoop) are very easy and inexpensive to make.

Make a deep-float leg float by tying a piece of light cord to the handle of an empty half-gallon plastic container (with a good top), such as a milk or juice container. Make the cord long enough so that a 4-inch loop at one end will hang 12 inches under water when the container is floating. You use the float by inserting one ankle into the loop. This will allow you to have some leg support at a depth of about 1 foot for some of the upcoming swimming drills.

You will need a safety float belt if you plan to try some deep-water drills without a trained lifeguard present. The float belt should be large enough to keep you afloat to chin level. Those few persons who are not buoyant (only 3% of the general population) will need a smaller float belt for the first few skills; the belt can be used for added confidence later on.

You can make a float belt by cutting blocks of closed-cell plastic foam, such as polyethylene, about 2 inches square and 6 to 8 inches long. Each of these blocks (you may need four or six of them) should be slit so that a 2-inch wide webbed nylon belt can pass through them. A belt of the type scuba divers use for a weight belt is ideal. You can also purchase a float belt, but do not buy one that is inflatable.

Hula hoops are useful in learning to dive. The hula hoop is a ring about 30 inches in diameter, usually made of rigid 1-inch plastic tubing. Make sure that your hula hoop floats. If it is plastic tubing, you may have to seal the joint where the ends meet so as to make it water tight. Attach a small weight to one point on the ring so that when immersed, it will stand on edge on the bottom of the pool. (You can purchase a hula hoop in many toy stores.)

For our friends in countries that use the metric system, the following conversion tables will simplify the distances and weights found in this book.

Inches × 2.54 = centimeters

Feet × 30.5 = centimeters

Feet × .304 = meters

Yards × .914 = meters

Pounds × .45 = kilograms

25 yds = 75 ft = 22.8 m

15 yds = 45 ft = 13.5 m

82 ft = 25 m

50 yds = 45.7 m

100 yds = 91.4 m

STEP 1

BUOYANCY: *EVERYONE* CAN FLOAT

E ven the most complicated swimming stroke involves only two basic skills: First, you float and, second, you add propulsive movements to move from place to place. "First you float" is the focus of Step 1. Floating is the basis of all swimming, and it's so easy you can't fail. In fact, for the vast majority of people, holding a full breath makes it impossible to sink even if they wanted to do so. When you discover that fact for yourself, you'll be well on your way to swimming. *Buoyancy* is an inherent body characteristic and does not need to be learned. Only about 3% of the general population have such heavy musculature and limited lung capacity that they can sink when immersed. Even the few nonbuoyant people can do a back float by adding small hand movements.

Learning to control the natural buoyancy of your body makes it easy to do a back float. Three important elements control buoyancy:

- Breath control (amount)
- Body position (balance)
- Relaxation

How to Prove That Your Body Floats

For your own safety and peace of mind, *always* have a skilled swimmer right beside you whenever you attempt a new skill.

Human bodies do not float *on* the water; they float *in* it! Only a specific percentage of the body will remain above the surface, and that percentage varies with every person. To discover how much of your body remains above the surface, find a place at the edge of the pool where the water is chin deep. Hold onto the side with two fingers of each hand and keep your stomach tight against the wall (see Figure 1.1a). Take a big breath, until your lungs are totally filled. Hold that breath, bend your knees so your feet are off the bottom, look straight forward (do not tilt your head back), and lower yourself *slowly* until only the very top of your head is above water (see Figure 1.1b). Bring both hands under the water momentarily (see Figure 1.1c).

You are floating!

Take hold of the edge and stand again.

FIGURE
1.1

BUOYANCY PROOF

Preparation

1. Head straight ___
2. Fingers on edge ___
3. Stomach tight against wall ___
4. Knees bent ___

a

5. Take *big* breath ___
6. Lower *slowly* ___
7. Hold that breath ___
8. Pull hands under water ___

b

9. Extend arms ___
10. Grasp edge ___
11. Stand ___

c

If you are one of those rare adults (usually male) who has neutral or negative buoyancy, we suggest that you wear a solid foam buoyancy belt that will give you enough positive buoyancy to float at eye level. The belt should be attached under the armpits, and the buoyancy should be circumferential, or split (see Figure 1.2). Wear the belt throughout Step 1.

Back Float

Now that you know your body is buoyant, you must be able to control that buoyancy to produce a body position that will allow you to breathe while you float. Most beginners attempt to float in a horizontal position and feel threatened when their legs drop to a natural, balanced floating position. Your balanced back-float position may be vertical, semivertical, or horizontal.

Why Is the Back Float Important?

The back float is one of the most important skills you will ever learn in swimming because it allows you to rest and breathe in deep water. It requires almost no effort and may save your life in the event of an aquatic emergency. The back float also teaches you how to balance your body in a close-to-horizontal position.

How to Float on Your Back

In chin-deep water assume the same starting position as for the buoyancy-proof float, but turn your face up to the ceiling and straighten your elbows to extend your arms fully (see Figure 1.3a). Be sure that your ears are fully submerged. Take a deep breath and hold it; release the edge and bring your hands underwater. Keep your eyes open as you drift slowly away from the wall (see Figure 1.3b). (Continue to wear a float belt through this skill if absolutely necessary. Position it as close as possible to lung position, split into two side floats.)

When you are steady in the water, *very quickly* exhale and inhale through your mouth. Take in a *full* breath. Hold that breath for 5 seconds, then quickly take another one. Remain perfectly still. Allow your knees to straighten. When you are confident, relax. *Slowly* bring your arms outward, underwater, until they are at shoulder height. Stop. Then continue very slowly to extend your arms upward

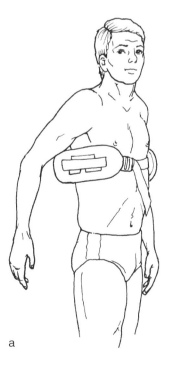
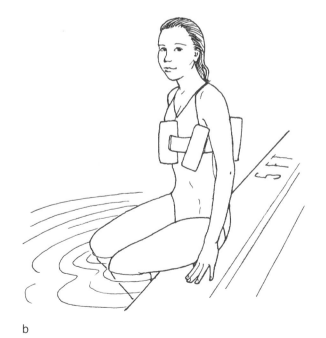

a   b

Figure 1.2 Buoyancy belts.

above your head. Keep them fully submerged (see Figure 1.3c). Your feet will rise as your arms move up. To recover: Bring your knees up, drop your chin forward, and sweep your arms downward behind you and forward past your hips, palms forward (see Figure 1.3d). Stay tucked until your feet are under you; then stand.

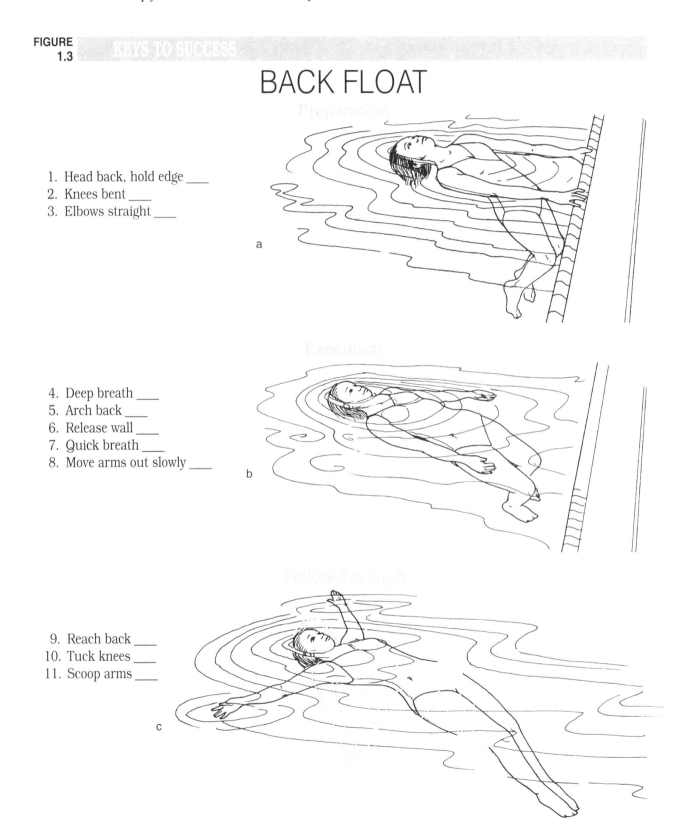

FIGURE 1.3

KEYS TO SUCCESS

BACK FLOAT

Preparation

1. Head back, hold edge ___
2. Knees bent ___
3. Elbows straight ___

a

Execution

4. Deep breath ___
5. Arch back ___
6. Release wall ___
7. Quick breath ___
8. Move arms out slowly ___

b

Follow-Through

9. Reach back ___
10. Tuck knees ___
11. Scoop arms ___

c

12. Vertical position ___
13. Stand ___

d

BUOYANCY SUCCESS STOPPERS

Learning the back float is very easy if you use the proper technique. Improper technique can make the process more difficult. Here are some common problems and ways to correct them.

Error	Correction
Buoyancy	
1. You tilt your head back.	1. Look straight ahead.
2. You are holding your body away from the wall.	2. Keep your elbows bent tightly.
3. Your head drops beneath the surface.	3. Lower your body *very* slowly. Take and hold *all the air you can hold.*
4. Your technique is correct, but your body still sinks.	4. Use a buoyancy belt temporarily.
Back Float	
1. Your face submerges.	1. Be sure you start with ears submerged and a full breath. (Need a float belt?)
2. Your hips drop.	2. Arch your back. Make a fat tummy.
3. Your face submerges on exhalation.	3. Exhale and inhale more quickly and fully. (Need a float belt?)
4. Your body stays nearly vertical.	4. Extend your arms higher overhead without bringing them out of the water.
5. You become tired.	5. Relax!
6. You become breathless.	6. Breathe more often.

DRILLS

To discover what percentage of your body remains above the surface, find a place at the edge of the pool where the water is chin deep (see Figure 1.1, p. 6). Hold onto the side with two fingers of each hand and keep your stomach tight against the wall. Fill your lungs completely. Hold that breath, bend your knees so your feet are off the bottom, look straight forward, and lower yourself *slowly* until the very top of your head is at the surface. Bring both hands under the water momentarily. YOU ARE FLOATING!

Take hold of the edge and stand again. Repeat this exercise several times. Try it with your eyes closed and with your eyes open.

Success Goal = 5 vertical floats with full confidence that your body will not sink and with some degree of relaxation ___

Success Check
• Take all the air you can hold ___
• Look straight ahead ___
• Lower very slowly ___
• Pull fingers under ___

To Increase Difficulty
• Push yourself under gently before releasing and float to the surface.

To Decrease Difficulty
• Try to take in even more air.
• Have a friend stand beside you for confidence.
• Wear goggles or a mask and look at the wall.
• Wear a small float belt.

Repeat the buoyancy discovery drill in deep water. Ask a skilled swimmer to stay beside you in the water to help you recover. Keep your knees straight.

Success Goal = 5 repetitions in deep water; hold for 15 seconds ___

Success Check
• Take in all the air you can hold ___
• Look straight ahead ___
• Lower body very slowly ___
• Pull fingers under ___

To Increase Difficulty
• Deliberately push yourself under and float to the surface.

To Decrease Difficulty
• Wear goggles or a mask and look at the wall.
• Hold your friend's hand with one hand.
• Wear a very small buoyancy belt.

3. Land Drill on Breathing

Correct breathing techniques are important to assure proper buoyancy and to enable you to hold a back float for more than one breath. This drill will prepare you to breathe while you float. Stand or sit on the edge of the pool. Take in all the air you can hold and hold it for just 5 seconds. Then exhale and inhale as quickly as possible through your mouth, making sure that you get *all* the air you can hold. Hold it for only 5 seconds; then exhale and inhale *quickly* again.

Total exhalation is not necessary; total inhalation is. Breathe "off the top of your lungs." Continue. See how quickly you can get a new breath. Open wide to breathe.

Success Goal = 20 breaths held only 5 seconds each and taken very quickly ___

Success Check
• Open mouth wide ___
• Exchange air quickly ___
• Fill lungs completely each time ___

To Increase Difficulty
• Hold each breath for 8 seconds.

To Decrease Difficulty
• Sit or stand erect; shoulders back.
• Breathe from your diaphragm; use your stomach muscles.
• Close your mouth while holding your breath.

4. Beginning Back Float

In chin-deep water with a friend standing directly behind you, place two fingers of each hand on the edge of the pool, turn your face up to the ceiling, and straighten your elbows to extend your arms fully. Be sure that your ears are fully submerged. Take a deep breath, hold it, release the edge, and bring your hands underwater. Keep your eyes open as you drift slowly away from the wall. When steady in the water, *very quickly* exhale and inhale through your mouth. Continue to breathe as in the previous drill. Remain perfectly still. Allow your knees to straighten. When you are confident, relax. *Slowly* bring your arms outward, underwater, until they are at shoulder height. Stop. Then continue very slowly to extend your arms upward above your head. Keep them fully submerged. Your feet will rise as your arms move up. To recover: Bring your knees up, drop your chin forward, and sweep your arms downward behind you and forward past your hips, palms forward. Stay tucked until your feet are under you and then stand (see Figure 1.3).

Success Goal = 5 consecutive floats and recoveries without submerging ___

Success Check
• Lungs fully inflated ___
• Back arched, arms out ___
• Breathe very quickly ___
• Move very slowly ___
• Tuck and scoop to recover ___

To Increase Difficulty
• Maintain your float for 3 minutes.
• When your arms are extended above shoulder height, pull them strongly back to your sides to move forward.

To Decrease Difficulty
• Have a friend hold one finger behind your neck as you recover.
• If you feel that your face is bobbing, hold each breath a little longer.
• Use a float belt.
• Use a nose clip to keep water out of your nose.

5. Deep-Water Back Float

With a skilled swimmer holding a large float belt in the water at your side, try the back float in deep water. Recover by taking hold of the float belt and kicking your way back to the edge.

Success Goal = 3 repetitions in deep water, holding float position and breathing for 30 seconds ___

Success Check
• Keep eyes open ___
• Breathe quickly, fully ___
• Move slowly ___

To Increase Difficulty
• Keep your arms at your sides and do a nearly vertical float with your chin fully extended.
• Maintain a deep water float for 3 minutes.

To Decrease Difficulty
• Wear a nose clip.
• Wear a float belt.

In chin-deep water, stand on the bottom, arms out at shoulder height, palms up. Tilt your head back until your ears are under water, take a deep breath, arch your back, and drift back into floating position. Do not try to lift your heels from the bottom. When you are floating, move your arms slowly overhead to raise your heels from the bottom. Breathe and hold the float as long as comfortable. Relax your body in this order: neck muscles, shoulder muscles, arm muscles, legs. Recover.

Success Goal = 3 successive floats and recoveries, 2 minutes each ___

Success Check
- Ears submerged ___
- Arms stretched overhead, submerged, until heels lift ___
- Hips up ___

To Increase Difficulty
- "Step" up to the surface with your feet while you float.
- Use your arms to pull yourself toward shallow water.

To Decrease Difficulty
- Have a friend stand directly behind you with one finger behind your neck to give you confidence.
- If your heels stay on the bottom, try bending your knees as you drift back.

BUOYANCY SUCCESS SUMMARY

You have mastered the hardest part of learning how to swim. You proved to yourself that your body is lighter than water when you hold your breath. You can breathe and control your buoyancy and body position in the water. This knowledge can be a lifesaver. If you fall into deep water, simply hold your breath until you surface, then go into a back float until you can attract attention and get help. Your clothing may actually hold enough air to help your float.

Ask an expert swimmer or an instructor to watch your back float and to make suggestions for improving it according to the keys to success in Figure 1.3.

STEP 2

SUPPORT AND PROPULSION:

ON THE MOVE

ou have learned that you have been endowed with the natural ability to remain at the surface of water just by breathing deeply and quickly. Now you need to learn how to move from place to place while you float. This step will show you how.

Pulling or pushing on the water while your body is floating is the basis of all forward motion in the water. Floating is effortless, and your arms or your legs can pull or push on the water as gently or as forcefully as you wish. Sculling and kicking for support and propulsion moves you through the water on your back.

Sculling

Sculling is an arm and hand motion that propels you through the water in a back-float position. It can also provide downward thrust to keep you at the surface. Adult males who are not buoyant must use sculling to keep their faces free of the water when they float on their backs. If you need a float belt for Step 1, try doing without the belt after a few sculling drills.

Why Is Sculling Important?

Sculling is the first propulsive movement you will learn. Sculling is important because it is the basis for all synchronized swimming figures and stunts and greatly increases a swimmer's sense of confidence and "water ability." All swimmers use some manner of sculling.

How to Scull

Start from a back-float position, arms just submerged along your side. Bend your wrists back slightly and keep your fingers together (see Figure 2.1a). Turn the heels of your hands and your wrists outward and move them away from your body about 15 inches (see Figure 2.1b). Then turn the heels of your hands inward and move them back to the starting position, making a figure-eight motion with your hands (see Figure 2.1c). Continue the figure-eight inward and outward movement without pause. The motion is exactly like polishing a vertical wall with your hands.

Nonbuoyant persons must hold their wrists nearly straight to apply downward pressure on the water.

FIGURE
2.1

KEYS TO SUCCESS

SCULLING

Preparation

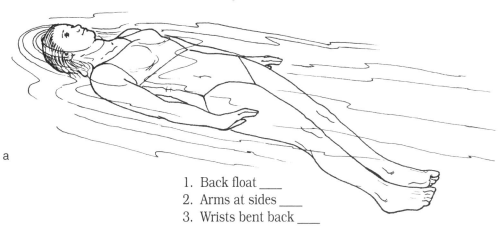

a

1. Back float ___
2. Arms at sides ___
3. Wrists bent back ___

Sculling Outward

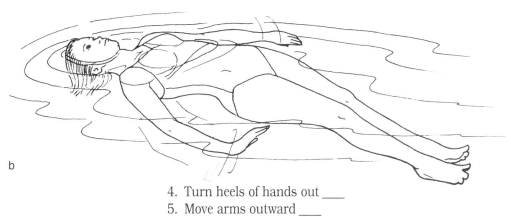

b

4. Turn heels of hands out ___
5. Move arms outward ___

Sculling Inward

c

6. Turn heels of hands in ___
7. Move arms inward ___

Support Kicking

Leg and foot motions in swimming serve three important functions: support, propulsion, and balance. The relative importance of these three functions varies greatly with the individual. Learners who have buoyant legs will need very little, if any, support from the leg and foot motion. They may spend less time on this skill and move on to back-crawl kicking.

Why Is Kicking Important?

For all swimmers and for all strokes, kicking supplies at least one of the functions listed above. Therefore, it is important to learn proper methods of leg and ankle motion and the variations within a kick that aid in determining which of the functions will be maximized. At this stage we are more interested in support than in propulsion.

How to Kick for Support

While sculling on your back, extend the toes of your right foot (see Figure 2.2a). Press downward on the water with the sole of your foot. Then draw your foot toward your body by bending at the knee and hip. Just before your knee breaks the surface, hook your ankle and step up to the surface (see Figure 2.2b). Your left leg and foot perform the same motions in opposition to the right leg. The result is *very* similar to pedaling a bicycle with emphasis on pressing the pedals downward with your toes extended (see Figure 2.2c). Keep your feet and knees under the surface. Your ankle should be hooked when moving upward and your foot should be pointed when moving downward as you press the water with the soles of your feet. Do not make a splash.

FIGURE 2.2

KEYS TO SUCCESS

SUPPORT KICKING

Sculling Position

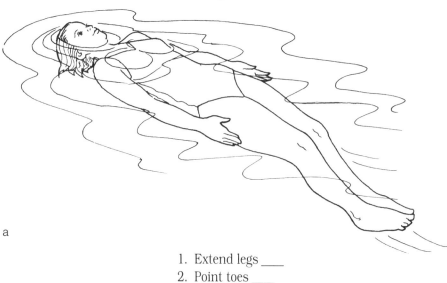

a

1. Extend legs ___
2. Point toes ___

Kicking

b

3. Press down with sole of right foot ___
4. Bring foot toward body; hook ankle ___
5. Step up to surface ___
6. Left leg presses as right leg recovers ___

Bike Motion

c

7. Ride-a-bike motion ___
8. Continue to circle ___

Another function of the kick in swimming is to propel the swimmer. Propulsion from your legs varies greatly with the type of kick and the flexibility of your ankles. In some strokes the kick supplies a major proportion of the propulsion; in others, the gain in propulsion may not be worth the expense in effort. Because it resembles the forward-back motion of walking, the back-crawl kick is the easiest kick to learn for propulsion in a back-float position. If your legs are so heavy that they do not come to the surface when sculling, you may wish to learn this kick while wearing a support belt at your hips.

This is the first propulsive movement of the legs you will learn. It is not a *necessary* motion for sculling, but rather an optional motion to aid in moving forward. There is a natural tendency to move the legs while swimming. If you don't need your legs for supporting movements, it is important to move them in an efficient, propulsive manner, rather than to allow them to cause resistance by dragging. This kick will also be important to you later, when you learn the back-crawl stroke.

Remember, though, that this kick can be tiring and is not the primary propulsive force while sculling. It uses a considerable amount of energy for the propulsion it produces. Use it sparingly and easily at this stage in your learning.

Start from a back-sculling position. Scull to bring your feet up near the surface (see Figure 2.3a). Your ankle must be *totally* relaxed. Drop one leg downward about 24 to 30 inches, keeping your other knee straight (see Figure 2.3b). Water pressure will force your ankle to hook during the downward motion. Move your leg upward again, allowing your knee to bend slightly as in a forward walking step. The upward movement will press your ankle into a pointed-toe position. Move your leg upward until your knee is just under the surface. Stop your knee at this point and straighten your leg. Your foot will "spoon" the water upward and backward, raising a mound of water (see Figure 2.3c). Move your other leg in the same manner, but in the opposite direction, causing an alternate upward and backward thrust of your feet against the water. If your ankle is truly relaxed, your toes will naturally turn slightly inward.

**FIGURE
2.3**

BACK-CRAWL KICKING

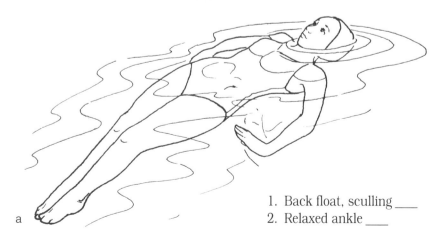

1. Back float, sculling ___
2. Relaxed ankle ___

a

Kicking

b

3. Drop one leg ___
4. Knee straight, foot hooks ___
5. Lift leg, knee bent 45 degrees ___
6. Straighten knee, flip water ___

Propulsion

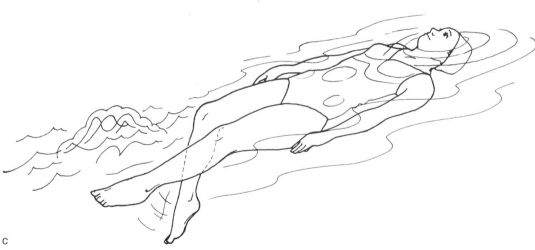

c

7. Legs alternate ___
8. Raise mound of water ___

Sculling and kicking for support and propulsion are not difficult; they just take a little practice. You will make some errors while learning. Use the corrections listed below to eliminate your problems.

Error	Correction
Sculling	
1. Your arms move out too far.	1. Move arms 15 inches only.
2. Your fingertips lead out and in.	2. Twist your arm from the shoulder; lead with the inside of your wrists.
3. You are sinking.	3. Take deeper breaths and hold 5 seconds.
4. You use proper technique, but you still sink.	4. Bend your wrists less, keep your fingers together, and apply downward pressure.
5. Your legs stay down.	5. Step gently up to the top.
6. Your arms/hands tire.	6. Relax your elbows/wrists.
7. You do not move forward.	7. Bend your wrist back more, twist your arms more.
Support Kicking	
1. Your hips sink to a sitting position.	1. Arch your back, push your hips up by pressing the sole of your foot downward.
2. Water splashes into your face.	2. Do not allow your knee or foot to break the surface.
3. Your legs sink while you kick.	3. Work your ankle. Point your toes while pressing; hook your ankle while lifting.
Back-Crawl Kicking	
1. Water splashes into your face.	1. Do not allow your knees to break the surface.
2. Your hips drop into sitting position	2. Arch; dig your toe in deeper before beginning to lift.
3. Your feet make a big splash.	3. Stop the upward flip of your toes before they break the surface.
4. You get little or no propulsion.	4. Relax your ankle and allow your foot to turn inward on the upthrust. Do not allow your knee to bend more than 45 degrees on the upthrust.

DRILLS

1. Sculling

Start from a back-float position in shallow water. Keep your arms a few inches under water along your side. Bend your wrists back, tilting your fingertips up. Keep your fingers together. Turn the heels of your hands and your wrists outward. Move them away from your body about 15 inches; turn the heels of your hands inward and move them back to the starting position, making a figure-eight motion with your hands. Feel the pressure on the palms of your hands as you press water toward your feet. Continue the figure-eight inward and outward movement without pause. The motion is exactly like polishing a vertical wall with your hands (see Figure 2.1).

Success Goal = 10 yards of head-first motion, hips remain at surface ___

Success Check
• Hips remain at the surface ___
• Move forward smoothly ___
• Hands move in and out, not up and down ___
• Arms rotate from shoulders ___

To Increase Difficulty
• Push off from the wall on your back and start sculling.

To Decrease Difficulty
• Wear a nose clip.
• Wear a float belt at your hips.

2. Variations on Sculling

Scull for distance. Do not try for speed. Practice making the sculling motions wider; then practice making them narrower. Try bending your elbows slightly.

Success Goal = 15 yards or across pool ___

Success Check
• Arms rotate from shoulder at each end of stroke ___
• Elbows bend slightly, wrists relax ___
• Feet remain at the surface ___

To Increase Difficulty
• Scull with your wrists straight, pressing down on the water.

To Decrease Difficulty
• Wear a small amount of buoyancy at your hips.
• Wear a nose clip.

A skilled swimmer holding a large float belt should swim beside you. Start in deep water and scull into shallow water. Scull for distance, not for speed.

Success Goal = 25 yards or 1 pool length ___

Success Check
• Steady, rhythmical movement ___
• Good forward progress ___

To Increase Difficulty
• Start in the middle of the pool and stay away from the edge.
• Discard the float belt if you used one.

To Decrease Difficulty
• Wear a small amount of buoyancy.
• Start from a wall and stay near the edge.

Start to scull in shallow water. Hold one arm still and scull with only one arm. You will discover that you will turn in a direction away from the sculling arm. Continue to turn a full circle.

Success Goal = 2 full circles in each direction ___

Success Check
• Smooth, continuous turn ___
• Opposite arm close to body ___
• No bend at hips ___

To Increase Difficulty
• Hold the nonsculling arm straight out from your shoulder and make a tight circle.
• Tighten your stomach muscles to kill your arch.

To Decrease Difficulty
• Wear a small amount of buoyancy.
• Make a large circle.

Ask a skilled swimmer to stay with you and to hold a large float belt. Start in shallow water a few feet from deep water. Scull into deep water. Stop sculling with one arm and turn until you are heading back into shallow water. Scull again with both arms until you return to shallow water. Repeat, turning in the other direction.

Success Goal = 5 turns in each direction ___

Success Check
• You are confident ___
• You do not need assistance ___

To Increase Difficulty
• Scull farther into deep water before turning.
• Stay in the middle of the pool, away from the sides.
• Make your turn tight and narrow.

To Decrease Difficulty
• Wear a small amount of buoyancy.
• Make the turn large.
• Stay close to the edge.

6. Sculling With Handicap

In shallow water, wear a 6-pound weight belt and scull across the pool.

Success Goal = wear a 6-pound belt and scull 15 yards ___

Success Check
- Scull steadily with no downward arm motions ___
- Keep feet together at the surface ___

To Increase Difficulty
- Wear a 10-pound belt.
- Scull and turn with weights.

To Decrease Difficulty
- Wear a 3-pound belt.
- Scull 10 yards.

7. Sculling for Speed

In shallow water race your buddy in sculling across the pool. Your hands must move in proper sculling form.

Success Goal = beating your buddy ___

Success Check
- Hands perpendicular to the line of motion ___
- Hands stay within 15 inches of legs ___

To Increase Difficulty
- Wear a weight belt.

To Decrease Difficulty
- Decrease the race distance.

8. Support Kick Against Wall

In shallow water with your back against the pool wall, stretch your arms out to the side and hook your elbows over the edge of the overflow trough. With your hips bent, extend your legs in front of you. Extend the toes of your right foot. Press downward on the water with the sole of your foot. Then draw your foot toward your body by bending at the knee and hip. Just before your knee breaks the surface, hook your ankle and step up to the surface. As the right foot steps up to the surface, press down with the left foot in the same manner. The result is *very* similar to pedaling a bicycle with emphasis on pressing the pedals downward with your toes extended. Step your feet upward to the surface. As your feet move up, arch your hips until your whole body is nearly horizontal. Do not allow your feet to break the surface (see Figure 2.2).

Success Goal = 5 times stepping to surface for 1 minute ___

Success Check
- Step your feet to the surface ___
- Raise hips until body is nearly horizontal ___
- Keep knees and feet under water ___

To Increase Difficulty
- Do a back float from standing position away from the side; then kick your feet and legs to the surface.

To Decrease Difficulty
- Have someone stand behind you and hold you under the armpits instead of hooking your arms on the side.

9. Support Kick With Kickboard

In shallow water hold a kickboard overhead. Lie back on the water. Keep your back arched and hips up. Use the support kick to step up to the surface. Avoid dropping your hips. Keep your chin up.

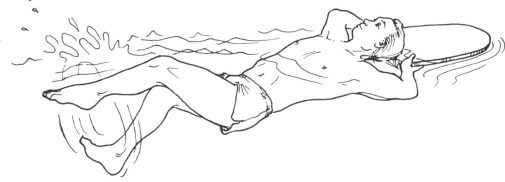

Success Goal = 3 minutes sustained horizontal position ___

Success Check
• Step your feet smoothly to the surface ___
• Maintain a horizontal position ___
• Do not splash ___

To Increase Difficulty
• Start in a back-float position with your arms overhead without the kickboard.

To Decrease Difficulty
• Have someone hold the kickboard.

10. Backstroke Kick Against Wall

In chest-deep water with your back against the pool wall, place your arms out to the sides. Keep your elbows on the top of the pool side or gutter. Grasp the edge with your hands and bend at the waist. Relax your ankles completely as you bring your legs up near the surface.

Drop one leg downward about 24 to 30 inches, keeping your knee straight. Water pressure will force your ankle to hook during the downward motion. Move your leg upward again and allow your knee to bend slightly. The upward movement will press your ankle into a pointed-toe position. Move your leg upward until your knee is just under the surface. Stop your knee at this point and straighten your leg. Your foot will spoon the water upward and backward, raising a mound of water. Move your other leg in the same manner, causing an alternate upward and backward thrust of your feet against the water. If your ankle is truly relaxed, your toes will naturally turn slightly inward.

Try to flip water up and back with your toes as if to splash someone standing beyond your feet. For this drill, actually splash water. Allow your ankles to be flexible and floppy. Count the upward thrusts (see Figure 2.3).

Success Goal = 30 upward thrusts; splashing ___

Success Check
• Keep your ankles loose and floppy ___
• Flip water up and back from your toes ___
• Keep your knees beneath the surface ___

To Increase Difficulty
• Start by splashing water. Gradually diminish the kick until only a mound of water is raised.

To Decrease Difficulty
• Instead of holding the side, have someone stand behind you and support you under your armpits.

11. Backstroke Kick With Kickboard

In shallow water hold a kickboard against your chest. Assume a back-float position. Lift your chin slightly. Kick upward and backward, but try not to produce a splash. Try, instead, to raise a mound of water above your feet as you kick. Emphasize the backward thrust and keep your hips at the surface. Move forward for distance.

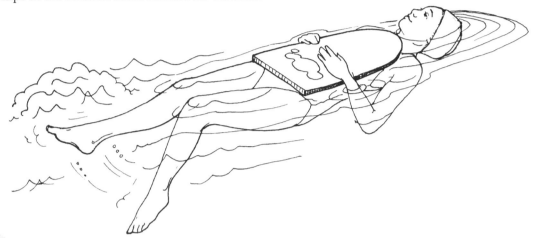

Success Goal = 15 yards forward movement __

Success Check
• Keep hips straight __
• Dig in with toe and lift __
• Raise a mound of water over your feet __

To Increase Difficulty
• Repeat the drill without the kickboard—hands at your side.
• Repeat the drill without the kickboard—hands overhead.

To Decrease Difficulty
• Think about the upward and backward pressure of the water on the tops of your feet.

12. Combined Scull and Kick

In shallow water assume a back-float position and begin to scull forward. Add either the support kick or backstroke kick. Continue to scull and kick across the pool.

Success Goal = 15 yards forward motion __

Success Check
• Keep hips at the surface __
• Keep knees just below the surface __
• Make little or no splash __

To Increase Difficulty
• Build up speed as you go.
• Wear a 3- to 5-pound weight belt.

To Decrease Difficulty
• Have a friend stay beside you.
• Stay near the edge of the pool.

In deep water with a skilled swimmer watching you, start a back float with sculling. Add either a support kick or a back-crawl kick and continue into shallow water. Lie back. Keep hips up.

Success Goal = 10 yards in deep water and 10 yards in shallow water ___

Success Check
• Very little splash ___
• Scull smoothly and rhythmically ___
• Breathe deeply and hold each breath momentarily ___

To Increase Difficulty
• Start in the middle of the pool.
• Have the skilled swimmer watch from the pool deck.
• Increase your distance in deep water.

To Decrease Difficulty
• Stay near the pool edge.
• Have the skilled swimmer in the water at your side.
• Start with a push-off from the pool edge.

Starting in shallow water with a skilled swimmer watching you, scull and kick into deep water. Continue to kick, but scull with one arm only as you make a wide turn and head back into shallow water. As you move toward shallow water, scull with both arms until you are in water of standing depth. Repeat, turning the other way.

Success Goal = 10 yards into deep water and return ___

Success Check
• Hips up ___
• No splash ___
• Expect to turn away from the sculling arm ___

To Increase Difficulty
• Start at the shallow end of the pool and go two full pool lengths.
• Turn 1-1/2 circles in deep water before starting back.

To Decrease Difficulty
• Have the skilled swimmer in the water beside you, holding a large float belt.
• Turn toward the nearest pool edge.
• Decrease the distance into deep water.

You have learned how to propel yourself from place to place in a back-float position. This is the essence of all swimming: First you float, and while you float, you pull or push yourself along.

Ask a skilled swimmer or instructor to compare your sculling and kicking to the keys-to-success checklists in Figures 2.1 to 2.3 and rate you on your smoothness and efficiency.

Now that you have seen how easy sculling and kicking really are, you are ready to try a full backstroke pull.

STEP 3

BASIC BACKSTROKE ARM PULL:
GO A MILE!

To be safe in the water, you need an alternative method for support and propulsion. You don't need to perform the back crawl as fast as Betsy Mitchell, who swims 100 meters in 53.98 seconds, or Rick Carey, who swims 200 yards in 1:44.43, but you do need skills that will enable you to swim for some distance without tiring. In addition, you should be able to change to a second method if you are bored with the stroke you're using. The basic backstroke arm pull is an excellent alternative to sculling. Sculling moves you through the water, but requires continuous motion. Several types of arm motions are possible with a backstroke. The basic backstroke arm pull is not only powerful, but also restful. It follows sculling in the most efficient learning progression.

Why Is the Basic Backstroke Arm Pull Important?

The basic backstroke arm motion propels you with considerable speed, and incorporates a long glide phase that allows you to rest between strokes. Some tired swimmers have actually saved their own lives with the basic backstroke arm motion when they were too fatigued to continue swimming any other stroke.

How to Perform the Basic Backstroke Arm Pull

Start the basic backstroke in the back-float position with your arms along your sides. Slide both your thumbs upward along your thighs, up your sides, and over your shoulders until your thumbs are touching the *top* of your shoulders (see Figure 3.1a). Your wrists should be fully flexed. Rotate your forearms until your fingertips point outward. Extend your arms—fingertips leading—and reach slightly above shoulder height (see Figure 3.1b). Take hold of the water with your hands and arms. Think about fastening your hands to the water at that point and pulling your body past your arms. Your feet will be a little lower than your head, so if your pull is level and just under the surface, your arms will finish the pull slightly in front of your body. After a good pull, you will be moving fast enough to coast and rest, gliding along in a streamlined back-float position with your arms down (see Figure 3.1c).

FIGURE
3.1   KEYS TO SUCCESS

BASIC BACKSTROKE ARM MOTION

Back Float

1. Float on back, arms at sides ___
2. Slide thumbs up sides to shoulder ___
3. Turn hands to point outward ___

a

Reach and Pull

4. Extend arms outward and upward ___
5. Stretch, just above shoulder height ___
6. Pull level toward feet ___

b

Glide

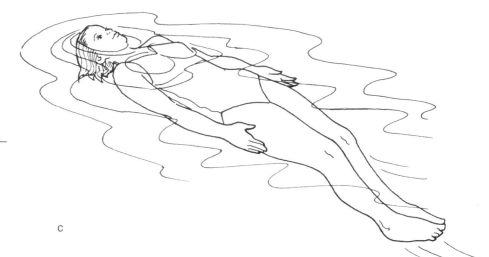

7. Arms at side ___
8. Relax; long glide ___

c

BASIC BACKSTROKE ARM PULL SUCCESS STOPPERS

It is important to perform this arm motion correctly because incorrect motions can result in splashing water in your face. Use the following list to correct the most common errors in the basic backstroke arm motions.

Error	Correction
1. Your hand starts moving outward before it reaches your shoulder.	1. Keep your thumb touching your side until it reaches the top of your shoulder.
2. The back of your hand leads as it moves out.	2. Rotate your lower arm at the elbow until your fingers point outward.
3. Your arm pull is too short.	3. Reach out above shoulder level. Stretch your arms way out.
4. Your body rises in the water, then sinks.	4. Pull level just under the surface.
5. Your head sinks during the pull.	5. Pull level not upward.
6. Water washes over your face while you pull.	6. Drop your chin slightly during the pull.
7. Water washes over your face while your arms recover.	7. Recover very slowly.

BASIC BACKSTROKE ARM PULL

DRILLS

1. Basic Backstroke Arm Pull

In shallow water at the edge of the pool, start the basic backstroke arm pull. Slide both your thumbs upward along your sides until your thumbs are touching the *top* of your shoulders. Rotate your forearm until your fingertips point outward. Extend your arms and reach out slightly above shoulder height. Take hold of the water with your hands and pull level and forcefully down toward your feet. Your feet will be a little deeper in the water than the rest of you, so your pull will finish slightly in front of your body. Stop and glide in a streamlined back-float position with your arms down. When your forward motion slows almost to a stop, recover and pull again. Continue across the pool; count how many strokes it takes to get across (see Figure 3.1).

Success Goal = 5 feet per stroke ___

Success Check
- Slide your thumbs all the way to the top of your shoulders ___
- Keep your hands and arms just under the water ___
- Make your pull long and strong ___
- Stop and glide after each pull ___
- Keep your hips up ___

To Increase Difficulty
- Try for a stronger pull and longer glide.
- Reach well above shoulder height on each pull.

To Decrease Difficulty
- Use a slow support kick.
- Wear a nose clip.

2. Deep-Water Backstroke Pull

Start in deep water and pull into shallow water. Make sure a skilled swimmer is watching your drill.

Success Goal = 25 yards or 1 pool length ___

Success Check
• Make long, full pulls ___
• Glide after each stroke ___
• Keep your arms under water ___
• Keep your hips up ___

To Increase Difficulty
• Stay in the middle of the pool.
• Ask a skilled swimmer to watch you from the side.

To Decrease Difficulty
• Stay close to the edge of the pool for confidence.
• Swim beside a skilled swimmer.
• Use a slow support kick while you pull.

3. Backstroke Pulls Plus Sculling

Start sculling in shallow water. After 20 feet change to the basic backstroke pull for the same distance. Kick if you wish.

Success Goal = 4 successful transitions ___

Success Check
• Make smooth transitions from sculling to pulling ___
• Keep your hands under water ___
• Keep your hips up at the surface ___

To Increase Difficulty
• Wear a weight belt.
• Continue kicking during the glide.
• Add a 90-degree turn during the sculling, but not toward deep water.

To Decrease Difficulty
• Use a support kick.
• Breathe deeply.
• Decrease the distance.

4. Deep-Water Backstroke

Start in deep water, scull toward shallow water, and add the back-crawl kick. After 10 yards change the sculling motion into a basic backstroke pull, and continue kicking and pulling into shallow water. A skilled swimmer should be watching.

Success Goal = 25 yards or 1 pool length ___

Success Check
• Swim with confidence ___
• Keep your hands beneath the water ___
• Generate very little splash ___
• Glide after each arm stroke ___

To Increase Difficulty
• Start in the middle of the pool.
• Eliminate the sculling and begin the backstroke immediately.

To Decrease Difficulty
• Swim beside a skilled swimmer.
• Stay close to the edge.

5. Swim and Turn

In shallow water swim with basic backstroke arm pulls and your choice of kick. Stop stroking with one arm at your side, but continue to pull with the other arm. You will turn in a direction away from the pulling arm. Continue to turn until you have completed a full circle. Then pull with both arms again. Stroke continuously—no glide during the turn. Repeat the drill with the other arm.

Success Goal = 3 complete circles ___

Success Check
- Keep your body straight and at the surface ___
- Do not splash with your feet ___
- Turn smoothly 360 degrees ___

To Increase Difficulty
- Turn half the circle, then shift to sculling to complete the circle.
- Decrease the number of arm pulls to turn.

To Decrease Difficulty
- Swim around a skilled swimmer, who stands at the center of the circle.

6. Deep-Water Swim and Turn

Start in shallow water. Swim backstroke into the deep water; then turn and swim back into shallow water. Kick and use arm strokes throughout the drill. A skilled swimmer should be watching.

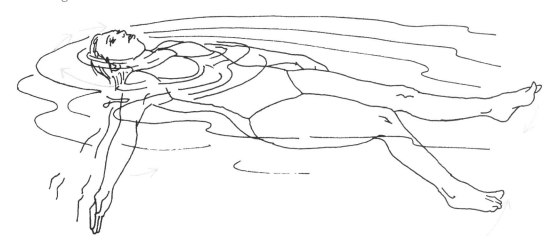

Success Goal = 5 deep-water turns in each direction ___

Success Check
- Stroke smoothly and rhythmically throughout ___
- Glide after each stroke when swimming straight ___
- Keep your hips at the surface while turning ___

To Increase Difficulty
- Swim from deep end to shallow end of the pool, turn, go back to deep end, turn, and return to shallow end.

To Decrease Difficulty
- Swim around a skilled swimmer in the deep water.

Backstroke is easy. If you take your time, swim slowly, and glide a lot, you could easily swim a mile. Try it! Use this table to start slowly, build your stamina and your confidence and really swim a mile non-stop.

In a 25-yard pool:
8.8 lengths = 1/8 mile
17.6 lengths = 1/4 mile
35.2 lengths = 1/2 mile
52.8 lengths = 3/4 mile
70.4 lengths = 1 mile

In a 25-meter pool:
8 lengths = 1/8 mile
16 lengths = 1/4 mile
32 lengths = 1/2 mile
48 lengths = 3/4 mile
64.3 lengths = 1 mile

Ask a skilled swimmer or instructor to compare your backstroke swimming with the keys to success in Figure 3.1 and rate your smoothness and efficiency.

STEP 4

MASK AND SNORKEL: ALMOST SKINDIVING!

The next step to success in swimming rests on the basic premise: You float—you push or pull—you are swimming! In this step, you'll be floating in a prone position (on your stomach so you can see where you're going) while you push or pull. Imagine you are swimming near your own tropical island, peering through your mask into the crystal waters. Breathe calmly through your snorkel as you watch the brilliant fish beneath you. You are about to enter the wonderful world of the mask and snorkel in which you float around on the surface and explore the scene below.

You start with a prone float, and before you know it you'll be almost skindiving (see Figure 4.1).

The Mask

A face mask should have a soft, flexible skirt that fits your face snugly, and it should have a face plate of safety glass or tempered glass. A face mask performs two functions: It keeps water from your eyes and nose, and it allows you to see clearly underwater.

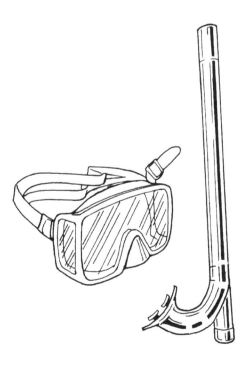

Figure 4.1 Mask, snorkel, and proper placement of this equipment for snorkeling.

Check the fit of a mask by placing it against your face without using the strap. Then inhale slightly to create suction. If the mask fits, it will remain on your face until you exhale. Keep the mask from fogging by applying two drops of dishwashing detergent to the inside of the glass. Rub it all around and rinse thoroughly at least twice.

Masks may be split into two separate eye pieces or consist of a single faceplate that can be round, oval, of rectangular. Let fit and comfort determine the shape you use.

The mask strap should be split into two sections so it will fit the back of your head better. It should have an easy-adjust mechanism at the side. Some masks come with built-in purge valves to clear water that leaks into the faceplate. Masks may even be purchased with prescription lenses, for those who need them.

Masks come in many colors and materials. Most have frames of colored plastic with skirts of black rubber or silicone compounds. Those with skirts made of silicone are translucent or clear, allowing more light into the mask. They are also less susceptible to damage from exposure to the sun.

The Snorkel

A snorkel should have a soft, flexible, curved section and a comfortable mouthpiece. When attached to the mask strap, it will fit comfortably in your mouth, remain upright while you swim, and allow you to breathe normally while your face is submerged. You can expel any water that inadvertently finds its way into the open end of the snorkel by puffing sharply into the snorkel to clear it. A little practice will allow you to clear your snorkel easily.

Snorkels come in various lengths but should never be more than 16 inches long. Those with purge valves near the mouthpiece (see Figure 4.1) are considerably easier to clear of extraneous water than those without.

Snorkel tube diameters also vary. In general, those with a wider bore diameter supply more air with less effort than the small bore type. Several attempts have been made to attach devices to snorkels to keep water from entering the top. None of them have been successful. Beginners should use only a basic snorkel with a purge valve.

Prone Float

You learned in previous steps that your body is lighter than water (or that you needed a small float belt). Your body retains its buoyancy regardless of the position you assume. It floats just as well face down as face up. That's common sense.

Prone Float and Recovery

The prone float is the basis for the most popular swimming strokes, such as the crawl stroke and the breaststroke. Remember, once again, that all swimming strokes are simply floating while you pull or push yourself through the water.

Put on your mask and snorkel and be sure to adjust them properly for comfort. Stand in shoulder-deep water and cautiously place your face in the water. Breathe normally through your mouth. Notice that you can see the bottom clearly and that breathing is easy. Take a few moments to get used to the sensation (see Figure 4.2a). Take a deep breath and hold it; then slowly slide your hands down the front of your legs to your ankles. You will notice that your feet want to leave the bottom (see Figure 4.2b). (Those who needed a float belt for the back float will also need it here.) Hold your breath as you fully extend your arms forward and your legs backward (see Figure 4.2c). Take a new breath very quickly and hold it. When you are ready to recover, bend at the waist to bring your legs back down, and put your hands on your knees again. Slide your hands back up to your thighs as you stand. Breathe.

FIGURE
4.2 KEYS TO SUCCESS

PRONE FLOAT
Preparation

1. Chest-deep water ___
2. Bend forward ___
3. Hands on thighs ___

a

Execution

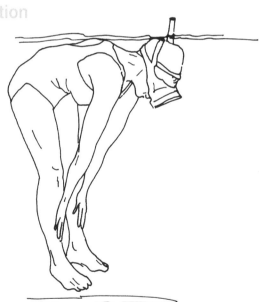

4. Breathe deeply ___
5. Face down ___
6. Slide hands to ankles ___
7. Extend arms and legs ___
8. Bend at waist to recover ___

b

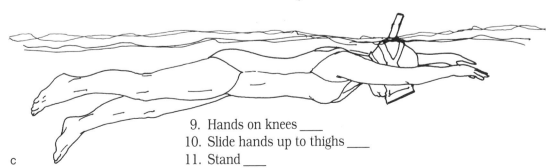

9. Hands on knees ___
10. Slide hands up to thighs ___
11. Stand ___

c

Bent-Knee Kick

The bent-knee kick is not an efficient kick, but it is selected here as the first kick for beginners because it seems to be an instinctive movement that requires little concentration to learn. It is also a close approximation to the very efficient crawl stroke kick, so the transition to the preferred kick will be easier when the time comes.

Beginners may reduce the amount of knee bend at any time in the learning process as it feels natural and as long as they continue to move their legs from the hips. Reducing the amount of knee bend may also help keep the feet underwater to increase efficiency.

You don't need the bent knee kick for a prone float because your feet will stay at or near the surface if you extend your arms fully forward while floating. There are, however, some important reasons for learning it now.

Why Is the Bent-Knee Kick Important?

Beginners invariably believe they must press down on the water to stay afloat. You have proven to yourself that this is not necessary. Yet, when you begin to make propulsive movements with your arms, you will almost certainly press downward somewhat. This downward pressure causes your feet and legs to sink rapidly in the prone position. You then need some kicking motion to counteract the downward press of the arms.

It is also very difficult to keep your legs still while your arms are moving. If your leg movement isn't correctly directed, it can be a major source of drag and will decrease the efficiency of your stroke. Furthermore, even though you can execute a prone float without a bent-knee kick, it will provide some measure of propulsion.

It is important to learn the bent-knee kick because it reduces the drag of your legs, keeps your feet from sinking, and produces some propulsive force.

How to Perform the Bent-Knee Kick

Wear a properly adjusted mask and snorkel. From a prone-float position with your face in the water (see Figure 4.3a), bend one knee and raise your foot and lower leg to a 90-degree angle behind you (see Figure 4.3b). Immediately kick your foot and lower leg downward again while raising the other one in a similar fashion (see Figure 4.3c). Alternately kick with one leg and then the other. A flexible ankle is vital because if the foot is hooked on the upward motion and extended on the downward motion, it will have a greater thrust in the downward direction, providing upward support. In addition, as the foot and lower leg extend from a 90-degree bend to a straight position, the backward force will provide some forward propulsion.

As you kick, try to make the kick progressively smaller until your feet stay mostly under the water.

FIGURE
4.3

KEYS TO SUCCESS

BENT-KNEE KICK

Preparation

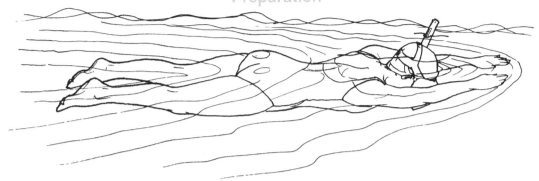

a

1. Prone float ___
2. Stretch arms overhead ___

Execution

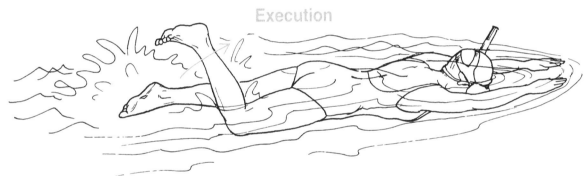

b

3. Bend one knee 90 degrees ___
4. Ankle relaxed, foot hooked ___

c

5. Kick down and back ___
6. Ankle relaxed, foot pointed ___
7. Repeat with other leg ___
8. Alternating, progressively smaller kicks ___

Even on something as easy as a prone float or a bent-knee kick errors can arise. They are easy to correct, however. Just apply the appropriate correction.

Error	Correction
Prone Float	
1. Your body sinks or your feet remain on the bottom.	1. Take a bigger breath. (Those who needed float belts for the back float will also need them now.)
2. You have trouble standing again.	2. Hold your hands on your knees until steady; stand.
3. You roll to one side while in extended position.	3. Do not arch your back. Spread your arms and legs slightly.
4. Your feet rise, then sink.	4. Stretch your arms; try to lift your hands above water.
5. You continue to roll over.	5. Bend forward slightly from the waist.
Bent-Knee Kick	
1. You do not move forward.	1. Bend your knee; kick back.
2. Your feet sink.	2. Flex your ankle; hook your foot on the up movement and point your foot on the down movement.
3. You make a big splash.	3. Narrow the kick; raise your chin.
4. You move backward.	4. Bend your knee more; shorten the downward thrust.
5. You kick mostly air.	5. Arch your back, push your chest out, raise your chin more.
6. You tend to roll.	6. Move your hands apart 2 feet.

DRILLS

1. Pick Up an Object

Adjust your mask and snorkel so the fit is snug and comfortable. Breathe through your mouth.

Stand in shoulder-deep water with the toes of one foot on a coin or any object that sinks. Put your hands on your thighs. Place your face in the water and breathe through your snorkel. Take a deep breath and hold it; slide your hands slowly down your legs and try to pick up the coin. Your feet will come up from the bottom, but you will not be able to get the object. Slide your hands back up your legs and stand.

Success Goal = prove to yourself that you cannot sink even if you want to do so ___

Success Check
• Move slowly ___
• Hold all the air you can take in ___
• Hang suspended like a jellyfish ___
• Slide hands back up to thighs ___

To Increase Difficulty
• Hold the jellyfish position for 10 seconds before standing.
• Perform the same drill without the mask and snorkel.

To Decrease Difficulty
• Have a friend stand directly in front of you for confidence.
• Wear a float belt *only* if you need it.

2. First Prone Float

Put on a mask and snorkel as shown in Figure 4.1. Stand in shoulder-deep water and place your face in the water. Breathe normally through your mouth. Take a deep breath and hold it, then slowly slide your hands down the front of your legs to your ankles. Your feet will float up from the bottom. (Use a float belt at your hips *only* if your feet stay on the bottom.)

Hold your breath as you fully extend your arms forward and your legs backward. Exhale and inhale a deep breath very quickly and hold it. When you are ready to recover, bend at the waist to bring your legs back down and put your hands on your knees. Slide your hands back up to your thighs as you stand. Breathe (see Figure 4.2).

Repeat the drill and count the seconds from the time you take the second breath.

Success Goal = 10 seconds in flat position ___

Success Check
• Hold a deep breath ___
• Slide hands down ___
• Watch your feet lift ___
• Stretch out flat ___
• Hands on knees ___
• Stand when steady ___

To Increase Difficulty
• Perform the drill on one breath without the mask and snorkel.

To Decrease Difficulty
• Take deeper breaths.
• Spread legs and arms slightly when extended.
• Don't try to stand until your hands are firmly on your knees.
• Have a friend stand directly in front of you to assist you to your feet.

3. Prone Float With Kickboard

Don your mask and snorkel. Stand in chest-deep water and hold a kickboard at arm's length in front of you with both hands. Take a deep breath and hold it, put your face in the water, and push off the bottom into a fully extended prone float. While floating, *lift* on the kickboard to keep your feet up. Take quick, deep breaths through your snorkel whenever you wish and hold each one. When you are ready to stand, press down on the kickboard and bring your legs down to vertical position before lifting your head.

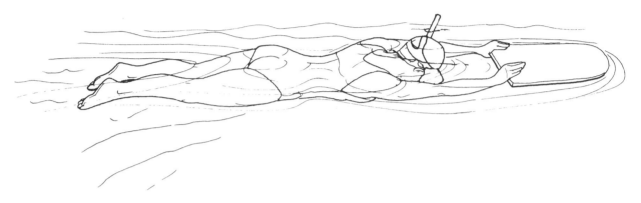

Success Goal = 1 minute in prone-float position ___

Success Check
- Push off gently ___
- *Lift* on the kickboard ___
- Breathe deeply and hold ___
- Press on the board until legs are down ___
- Lift head and stand ___

To Increase Difficulty
- Perform the drill for 20 seconds without the mask and snorkel.
- Increase the time with mask and snorkel to 2 minutes.

To Decrease Difficulty
- Keep your legs slightly apart.
- Decrease the float time.
- Concentrate on keeping your lungs full.

4. Prone Float With Kickboard, Head up

Repeat Drill 3, but try to do the float with your head up, facing forward. Note that keeping your head up requires downward pressure on the kickboard, which in turn causes your feet to sink rapidly.

Success Goal = Realization that you cannot remain in a prone position with your head up.

Success Check
- Raise your head ___
- Press on the board ___
- Feel your feet sink ___

5. Prone Float and Glide With Kickboard

Don your mask and snorkel and stand with your back against the wall. Hold a kickboard with both hands at arm's length in front of you. Place one foot behind you against the wall and put your face in the water. Push off the wall into prone float position, streamlining your body (especially your feet and toes), and *lift* on the board. Stretch and hold this position until your forward glide stops. Breathe deeply and quickly if necessary. Press on the board to stand.

Success Goal = 5-yard glide ___

Success Check
- Powerful, level pushoff ___
- Legs together, toes pointed, body straight ___
- Lift on kickboard ___
- Long glide to stop ___

To Increase Difficulty
- Eliminate the mask and snorkel.

To Decrease Difficulty
- Work on streamlining.
- Decrease the expected glide length.
- Get your foot up high on the wall for a level push.

6. Prone Float and Glide Without Kickboard

Repeat Drill 5 without the kickboard. Keep your arms fully extended and lift your hands to the very top of the water. When your glide is finished, press forcefully downward with both hands while drawing your knees into a tight tuck. Keep pressing until you are upright before attempting to put your feet down.

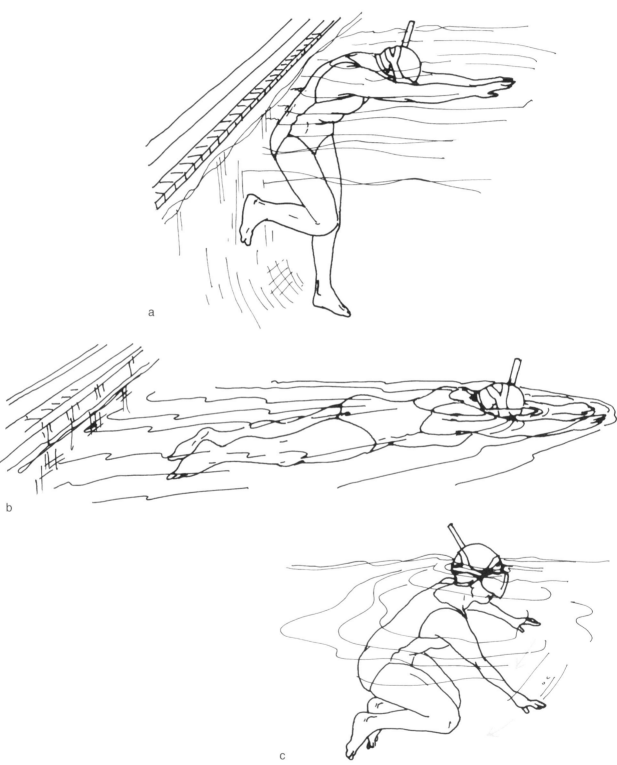

a

b

c

Success Goal = 20-foot glide ___

Success Check
• Streamline ___
• Lift hands and arms ___
• Press and tuck knees simultaneously ___

To Increase Difficulty
• Eliminate the mask and snorkel.

To Decrease Difficulty
• Have a friend stand by to assist with recovery.
• Decrease the glide distance.

7. Float and Bent-Knee Kick

Wear a properly fitted mask and snorkel. From a prone-float position with your face in the water, bend one knee and raise your foot and lower leg to a 90-degree angle behind you. Immediately kick the foot and lower leg downward again while raising the other one in a similar fashion. Alternately kick with one leg and then the other. Relax your ankles and let your feet flop. Try to keep your lungs full by breathing deeply and holding each breath. Raise your chin to help keep the kick under water. Kicking air is not productive. Watch the bottom to see your forward progress. Continue to kick for 20 feet (see Figure 4.3, p. 37).

Success Goal = 20-foot forward progress

Success Check
• Extend arms in front ___
• Raise chin, look forward under water ___
• Press backward with top of foot ___
• Kick mostly under water ___

To Increase Difficulty
• Eliminate the mask and snorkel.
• Increase the distance goal.

To Decrease Difficulty
• Stay close to the pool edge.
• Tuck your knees and press down to recover.
• Have a friend ready to assist you to recover.

8. Bent-Knee Kick and Breathing With a Kickboard

Try this drill without a mask and snorkel. In shallow water, hold a kickboard at arm's length, take a deep breath and hold it, put your face in the water, and push off the side of the pool. Start kicking. When you need a breath, press on the kickboard, thrust your chin forward, and exhale and inhale through your mouth. Drop your face into the water and lift on the kickboard as you continue. Avoid l*ifting* your head to breathe. Try to keep your chin at water level as you take a breath.

Success Goal = 15 yards on 3 breaths ___

Success Check
• Kick steadily while breathing ___
• Tilt head back, don't lift it ___
• Breathe quickly, deeply through mouth ___
• Drop face in, hold breath ___

To Increase Difficulty
• Do not hold your breath. Exhale as your face submerges and thrust your chin forward for another breath immediately.

To Decrease Difficulty
• Decrease the distance.
• Wear a mask or goggles without the snorkel.

9. Bent-Knee Kick and Breathing Without Kickboard, Mask, or Snorkel

In shallow water, push off the side of the pool in prone-float position and begin kicking. When you need a breath, scull and press down with your hands as you thrust your chin forward long enough to get a quick breath. Avoid lifting your head; keep your chin at water level. Exhale and inhale quickly through your mouth and drop your face back into the water.

Success Goal = 3 successful breaths __

Success Check
• Thrust chin forward, don't lift head __
• Exhale and inhale quickly __
• Drop face back into water __

To Increase Difficulty
• Raise the goal to four or five breaths.

To Decrease Difficulty
• Decrease the goal to two successful breaths.
• Wear a mask or goggles without a snorkel.
• Turn your face to the side, ear on the water, for your breath.

10. Bent-Knee Kick and Breathing, Head up

Use a kickboard, but no mask or snorkel. Hold a kickboard at arm's length in shallow water. Push off the wall, but hold your chin at water level so you can breathe whenever you wish. Notice the tendency for your feet to sink. The harder you press on the board or the higher you raise your chin, the more your feet will drop.

Success Goal = 15 yards __

Success Check
• Chin at water level __
• Breathe quickly, hold each breath __
• Kick near the surface __

To Increase Difficulty
• Do not use a kickboard. Scull and press on the water with your hands to keep your head up.

To Decrease Difficulty
• Use two kickboards.
• Turn your face to the side, keep your ear on the water to breathe.
• Bring the kickboard in and rest your chin on it.

11. Bent-Knee Kick for Extra Support

Hold on to the side of the pool or a ladder at water level and kick. As you kick, press on your hands until your head and neck are above water (water at shoulder level). Note how your feet sink. Kick harder to keep them up while your neck and head are out of the water. See how long you can maintain this position.

Success Goal = 30 seconds ___

Success Check
• Keep arms straight ___
• Look forward ___
• Kick hard ___

To Increase Difficulty
• Don't even try!

To Decrease Difficulty
• Cheat!
• Stay a little lower in the water.
• Bend your elbows a little.

12. Bent-Knee Kick Evaluation

Press very hard on a kickboard while kicking in the prone position. Try to raise your head and shoulders high, still keeping your feet at the surface. Then hold the board at arm's length and put your face in the water as you kick. Compare the amount of energy used each way.

Draw conclusions about whether a kick is an efficient way to keep your head out of the water and whether it is profitable to press downward on the water while swimming.

Success Goal = realization that pressing downward on the water consumes a lot of energy for minimal results. (Isn't it better to just float and pull or push?) ___

MASK AND SNORKEL SUCCESS SUMMARY

To be sure that you are performing the prone float and kicking correctly have a swimming expert or instructor check your skills against the descriptions in Figures 4.2 and 4.3.

You have learned a lot in Step 4: that your body is equally buoyant in any position, that you can do a prone float easily, that kicking can provide support as well as propulsion, and that masks and snorkels make swimming easier. You have also learned that downward pressure on the water is wasted effort and that you need more instruction on how to breathe when swimming without a snorkel. You have even sampled the great joys of skindiving. You are ready now to do some actual face-down swimming. It's easy!

STEP
5

KICK AND PULL:

YOU'RE SWIMMING NOW!

You know that your body will float without effort. You know that you can make some forward progress and keep your feet up by kicking. If you wear a mask and snorkel, you can see the pool bottom clearly and breathe easily with your face in the water. You have not yet, however, tapped the major source of propulsion: pulling.

Basic Armstroke

In this step you will combine the propulsive movements of your legs with the basic armstroke that will, in fact, enable you to swim quite well in a face-down position. You will make a giant step forward in your ability to be safe in the water and to swim almost anywhere.

Why Is the Basic Armstroke Important?

The basic armstroke is a transition arm stroke. It is important because it allows you to move forward through the water while you remain in a stable face-down position and because it teaches you the fundamentals of using your hands and forearms for propulsion. Attempting the more efficient crawl arm stroke at this point would disrupt your balance and body position.

How to Execute the Basic Armstroke

Start from a prone glide position. Wear your mask and snorkel. Extend your arms forward and flex your right wrist so your fingers point downward with the palm facing back. Begin the pull with forearm and hand; keep your elbow high. Bend the elbow so your hand and forearm move inward and backward. Straighten your wrist as your forearm moves. Your hand should now be in the center line of your body directly under your nose—elbow bent 90 degrees, wrist straight (see Figure 5.1a). Push water directly back under your body with the hand about 6 inches from your chest. As you push past your waist, straighten your elbow and allow your hand to move outward to your right thigh (see Figure 5.1b). When your thumb touches your thigh, begin the recovery by keeping your elbow close as you draw the hand along your body to the chin; then turn your palm down and push your hand forward, fingers leading, to full-arm extension (see Figure 5.1c). Pause. Transfer your attention to your left arm.

Repeat the motion with your left arm.

FIGURE 5.1

BASIC ARMSTROKE

Preparation

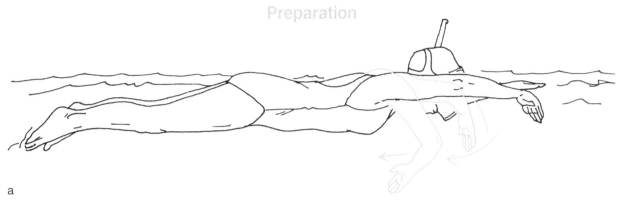

a

1. Prone glide; arms overhead ___
2. Flex wrist; hold elbow high ___
3. Bend elbow 90 degrees ___

Execution

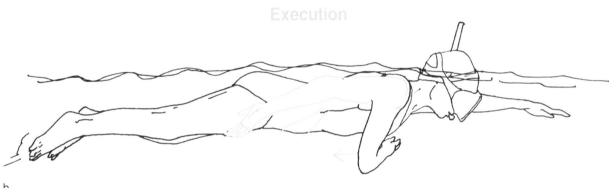

b

4. Pull back with right hand ___
5. Horizontal pull under body ___
6. Thumb touches thigh ___
7. Recover close to body ___
8. Extend right arm ___

Recovery

c

9. Same pull with left hand ___
10. Alternate pulls ___

There are a number of errors that can make this pull inefficient. Use the correction list to counteract your errors.

Error	Correction
1. Your pull is too deep.	1. Bend the elbow 90 degrees to keep your forearm horizontal; keep hand about 6 inches under your body.
2. Your feet sink quickly.	2. Pull with your arm only, not with body muscles.
3. Your feet sink slowly.	3. Do not press downward on the water. Push the water directly backward.
4. You push water on the recovery.	4. Keep your hand close to your body.
5. You start to pull with one arm before the other is completely finished.	5. Make one hand touch the other before starting the next pull.

DRILLS

1. Basic Armstroke With Mask and Snorkel

In shallow water, wearing your mask and snorkel, push off from a wall and glide. When your glide slows, begin pulling with your arms (see Figure 5.1). Concentrate on long, full pulls; reach all the way back until your thumb touches your thigh. Be sure to pull and push backward on the water without pushing downward. Do not even think about your feet; let them do whatever they want.

Success Goal = 15 yards ___

Success Check
- Take long, full pulls ___
- Keep feet near the surface ___
- Sneak arms forward close to body ___
- Finish one arm and stretch before starting next ___
- Make significant progress on each pull ___

To Increase Difficulty
- Inhale while pulling with one arm and exhale while pulling with the other.
- Use a bent-knee kick while pulling.

To Decrease Difficulty
- Decrease the distance.
- Hold a leg float between your knees.

2. Turning With Basic Armstroke: Mask, Snorkel, and Leg Float

Hold a pull-buoy (leg float) between your knees, use a mask and snorkel, and practice the basic armstroke. Be sure each pull is full length. After four pulls, look and reach to the left on each pull to make a left turn. Continue pulling, but look and reach to the right on each pull to make a right turn.

Success Goal = a 180-degree turn in each direction ___

Success Check
- Turn head to look in the direction of the turn ___
- Pull body around with reaching arm ___
- Pull all the way to your leg ___

To Increase Difficulty
- Use a bent-knee kick instead of a leg float.
- Inhale on one arm pull (left or right) and exhale on the other. Always inhale on the same arm pull.
- Pull and turn without a mask and snorkel. Keep your face down, hold your breath, thrust your chin forward to get another breath.

To Decrease Difficulty
- Reduce each turn to 90 degrees.
- Have a friend stand as a goal to turn around.

3. Turning With Basic Armstroke: Mask and Snorkel Only

Repeat Drill 2 without the leg float. If your feet sink, correct your pull so there is no downward pressure. All the force should be directed backward toward your feet. Use the bent-knee kick if you wish.

Success Goal = alternating 4 left and 4 right 90-degree turns without stopping ___

Success Check
- Pull level, not downward ___
- Allow your feet and legs to float ___
- Keep any kick small ___

To Increase Difficulty
- Drill without a mask and snorkel. Keep your face down, hold your breath, and get a new breath when needed.

To Decrease Difficulty
- Swim slowly, don't fight it.
- Keep your lungs well inflated; deep breaths.

*4. Deep-Water Turns and Basic Armstroke
With Mask, Snorkel, and Safety Float*

Have a good swimmer with you; wear a safety float at your waist instead of a leg float. Pull from shallow water into deep water, do a wide turn, and return to shallow water. Use the bent-knee kick to help keep your legs up and for propulsion.

CAUTION: Do *NOT* attempt this drill without a safety float unless you are accompanied by a trained lifesaver!

Success Goal = 4 round trips with rests between ___

Success Check

- Use long pulls ___
- Keep your kick small ___
- Finish each arm pull before beginning the next ___
- Swim slowly; float along and pull ___

To Increase Difficulty

- Swim a full circle in deep water before starting back.
- Make turns in both directions.
- Eliminate the mask and snorkel. Hold each breath and keep your face down except when breathing.

To Decrease Difficulty

- Make the deep-water part short.
- Make two trips.

KICK AND PULL SUCCESS SUMMARY

Wow! You're swimming! You should feel quite confident about your ability to stay at the surface and to get from place to place fairly well. You should even be feeling somewhat more comfortable in deep water because you know you can move around.

To understand just how well you are progressing, get a second opinion. Have a swimming instructor or a knowledgeable friend evaluate your basic armstroke and kick by comparing them with the keys to success in Figure 5.1 and Figure 4.3. Then work a little more on any weak points.

It has been nice to be able to breathe through a snorkel while learning, but now it is time to learn that you can also breathe without the snorkel. The next step will teach you how to get a breath when you need it.

STEP 6

BREATHING: NEW APPROACH TO OLD HABIT

Karen and Sarah, the Josephson twins, won an Olympic gold medal in synchronized swimming. Did you watch them on television? Did it seem to you that they must have gills instead of lungs? They stayed under the water for what seems like an impossible length of time while performing their stunts and figures.

Breath control is an essential ingredient in all swimming. Recreational swimmers, speed swimmers, and synchronized swimmers all need to learn correct breathing habits to be good at what they do. This step shows you how to integrate breath control into prone-swimming techniques.

Why Is Breath Control Important?

Learning to control your breathing to make it fit your swimming stroke pattern is probably the most difficult and the most rewarding skill required in the sport of swimming. You must practice breath control until it becomes a habit. When you have become truly proficient, you will probably find yourself practicing swimming breathing patterns involuntarily every time you step into a shower. Correct breathing patterns differentiate the polished, expert swimmer from the novice. *Correct breath control habits are vital to swimming.*

About Breathing

In swimming you cannot breathe when you want to—you must breathe when you can. Often, the rhythm of a stroke allows only a very short breathing time.

Your nose is not large enough to allow you to take in the amount of air you require in the short interval. You can solve this problem by breathing through your mouth. Exhaling through your nose is important because it helps to keep the water out, but the volume of air you must exhale in the time allowed requires that you exhale partly through your mouth as well.

Your buoyancy depends upon the amount of air in your lungs. You cannot hold a full breath all the time you are swimming, but you can keep your lungs more nearly inflated by inhaling fully and exhaling about half the air on each breath. Thus you can "breathe off the top of your lungs." If this technique leaves you breathless, you must revert to full and complete exhalations and inhalations

This step leads you through a series of drills that establishes proper breathing techniques gradually.

How to Control Your Breathing While Swimming

Start by lying prone in the water. Hold onto the edge of the pool with both hands with a float between your knees. Take a breath through your mouth and place your face in the water. Look slightly forward so the water line is on your forehead. Exhale fully through your nose. The air will come out easier if you "hum" it out using your voice. After exhaling completely, turn your head to the side until your mouth is just at water level. Do not *lift* your head, but leave your ear in the water. Open your mouth wide, inhale quickly, and turn your face into the water again to exhale (see Figure 6.1).

FIGURE
6.1 KEYS TO SUCCESS

BREATHING

Preparation

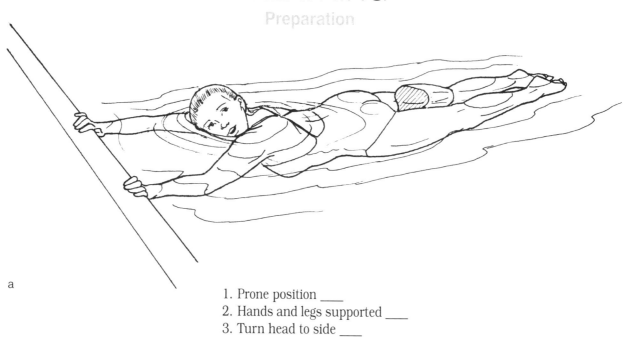

a

1. Prone position ___
2. Hands and legs supported ___
3. Turn head to side ___

Execution

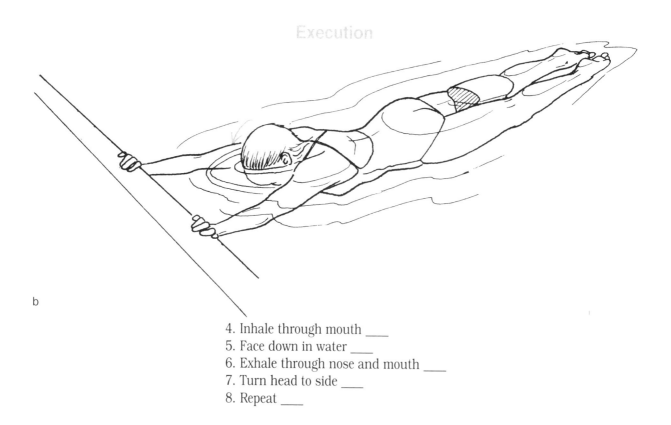

b

4. Inhale through mouth ___
5. Face down in water ___
6. Exhale through nose and mouth ___
7. Turn head to side ___
8. Repeat ___

Pulling and Breathing

During the pulling and breathing exercises, you will probably discover that it seems easier to breathe on one side than on the other. Most people have a favorite breathing side. In the drills for this section we refer to your favorite side as your "breathing side." In addition, in this and many subsequent drill sequences, you will be using the deep-float leg support mentioned in the equipment list at the beginning of the book (see Figure 6.2).

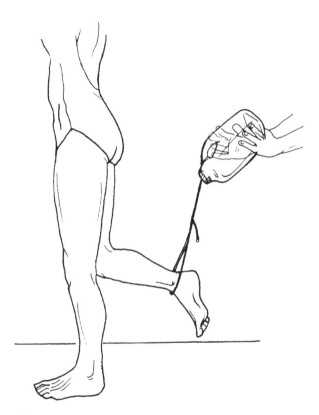

Figure 6.2 Deep-float leg support.

At this point you know how to pull and how to breathe. Combining the two skills (and possibly a third—kicking) adds a new element to breath control: timing. Until this point, you were free to breathe at any time you felt the need. Now you will learn to make your breathing fit the timing of your stroke, rather than stroking to fit your breathing.

Why Is This Two-Skill Combination Important?

The most efficient and the fastest swim stroke we know is the crawl stroke. The crawl is the essence of swimming, the stroke everyone visualizes when they hear the the word *swimming*. You won't be an accomplished swimmer until you can do the crawl stroke well. You are on your way to learning it now, but it requires rhythmic breathing matched to your arm stroke. This two-skill combination is the point at which most novice swimmers stumble. If you follow the drill sequence, you will breeze through this traditional stumbling point with very little difficulty and be well on your way to successful swimming.

How to Pull and Breathe

Assume a prone position while pulling. Exhale until the arm on your *breathing side* begins to pull (see Figure 6.3a). Begin to turn your head up for a breath while the arm is making the first half of its pull. The mouth should then be free to take a breath during the last half of the pull (see Figure 6.3b). Take a quick but full breath and return your face to the water as the arm begins its recovery. Exhale during the pull and recovery of the non-breathing-side arm as shown

FIGURE
6.3

PULLING AND BREATHING

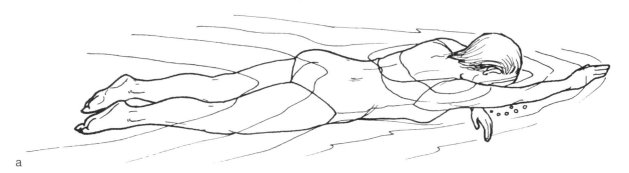

a

1. Prone position, pulling ___
2. Exhale during nonbreathing pull with face down ___

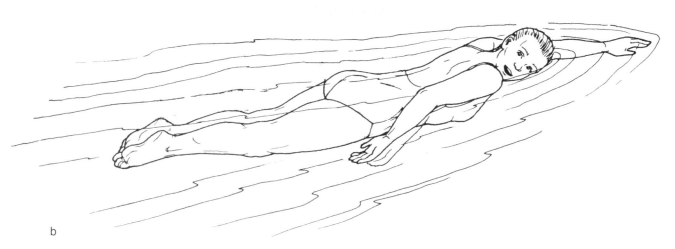

b

3. Roll face to side during first half of arm pull on the breathing side ___
4. Breathe during the second half of the arm pull on the breathing side ___

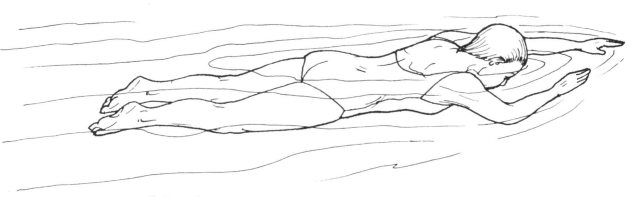

c

5. Turn face down during recovery of breathing-side arm ___
6. Repeat ___

BREATHING SUCCESS STOPPERS

Breathing in the water is a precise skill. It is normal to have trouble with it at first. Here are some problems you may encounter and ways to fix them.

ERROR	CORRECTION
Breathing	
1. Water gets in your nose when your face is down.	1. Keep the waterline at your forehead. Exhale partly through your nose.
2. Your head and shoulders are above water while you inhale.	2. Turn your head instead of lifting it. Keep your ear under water.
3. You have difficulty exhaling fully.	3. Use your voice. Hum.
4. Your feet tend to sink.	4. Put less pressure on your hands. Keep your head lower.
5. You get breathless during continued breathing.	5. Exhale fully and inhale deeply.
Pulling and Breathing	
1. Your arm interferes because you breathe too early.	1. Turn your head but do not breathe during the first half of the pull.
2. You breathe too late while your face is rolling down.	2. Breathe during the last half of the pull.
3. Your timing is right, but you breathe water.	3. Roll farther to the side to get your mouth clear.
4. Your feet sink.	4. Roll your head; do not lift it. Do not press downward with your hands.

BREATHING

DRILLS

1. Bracket and Leg Float, Side Breathing

Hold onto the side of the pool with both hands. Use a leg float to support your legs. Turn your head to one side, lay your ear on the water, and keep your mouth at water level. Inhale through your mouth, turn your face down, and exhale through your nose. Continue breathing to the side. If you have difficulty, do not lift your head. Instead leave your ear on the water and turn your head farther (roll your shoulders).

Success Goal = 10 consecutive breaths ___

Success Check
• Keep your ear in the water ___
• Inhale quickly ___
• Exhale slowly ___

To Increase Difficulty
• Discard the leg float.
• Try 20 consecutive breaths.
• Let go of the edge, press with the breathing-side arm to roll your body to breathe.

To Decrease Difficulty
• Move your arms a little farther apart.
• Hum the air out.
• If you get water in your nose, time your exhalation so you are still humming as your nose breaks the surface.

2. Rhythmic Side Breathing, Floating With Kickboard

Hold a kickboard at arm's length in front of you. Use a leg float. Do not try to move forward, just float motionless. Turn your head to one side, laying your ear on the water. Take a quick breath and turn your face down to exhale through your nose. Lift on the kickboard as you exhale to keep your feet up.

Success Goal = 10 consecutive breaths ___

Success Check
• Keep your ear under water ___
• Inhale through your mouth ___
• Hum the air out slowly ___

To Increase Difficulty
• Take 20 consecutive breaths.
• Release the board and scull while breathing.

To Decrease Difficulty
• Take the breathing-side arm off the kickboard and press on the water while you inhale.
• Wear goggles.

3. Rhythmic Side Breathing, Floating and Kicking

Hold a kickboard at arm's length in front of you while you float face downward. Kick your legs for support and breathe rhythmically to the side. Remove your breathing-side hand from the kickboard if it gets in your way, but replace it during exhalation.

Success Goal = 10 consecutive breaths ___

Success Check
• Use a small kick ___
• Keep your ear on the water ___
• Inhale quickly through your mouth ___
• Exhale slowly through your nose ___

To Increase Difficulty
• Discard the board and scull with both hands.
• Take 20 consecutive breaths.

To Decrease Difficulty
• Scull with your breathing-side arm while inhaling.
• Roll your shoulder and your face up to inhale.

4. Rhythmic Side-Breathing for Distance

With a kickboard, kick while inhaling on the side and exhaling face down. Do not count breaths, but continue as long as you can breathe comfortably. Keep your ear on the water. Turn your head without lifting.

Success Goal = 15 yards ___

Success Check
• Keep your ear under water ___
• Inhale quickly through your mouth___
• Exhale slowly through your nose ___
• Small kick ___

To Increase Difficulty
• Discard the board and scull with your hands.
• Breathe on alternate sides.

To Decrease Difficulty
• Remove your breathing-side arm from the board and scull with it.
• Lift on the board while exhaling.
• Wear goggles.

Don a mask, snorkel, and deep-leg float. Do a prone float and basic armstroke, but change the emphasis. Concentrate on timing your breathing to your stroke. Inhale *only* during the pull of the arm on your breathing side; exhale (through your mouth) *only* during the pull of the opposite arm. Do not hold your breath at any time. Breathe on *every* breathing-side arm pull and exhale on *every* opposite-arm pull. Keep your face down. Do not try to kick. Keep your feet together.

Success Goal = 20 consecutive pulls with breathing ___

Success Check
- Pull slowly to match your breathing rhythm ___
- Inhale during the breathing-arm pull ___
- Exhale during the opposite-arm pull ___
- Keep your feet still ___

To Increase Difficulty
- Discard the float and kick while pulling.
- Try to inhale on the pull and hold your breath while that arm recovers; then exhale slowly while the other arm pulls *and* recovers.

To Decrease Difficulty
- Use a pull-buoy leg float instead of the deep float.
- Finish each stroke completely before starting the next.

Do not use a mask or snorkel. Attach a deep float to the ankle on your breathing side. Assume a floating position. Keep your feet together and start by exhaling as you pull with the non-breathing-side arm. Then turn your head to the breathing-side and inhale with the pull of your breathing-side arm. Leave your ear under water. Turn your face back down to exhale while you pull with the opposite arm. Continue to pull and breathe.

a

b

Success Goal = 10 consecutive breaths while pulling ___

Success Check
- Finish each arm pull before beginning the next ___
- Exhale through your nose ___
- Inhale through wide mouth ___
- Keep your ear on the water ___

To Increase Difficulty
- Discard the float; kick.
- Try for 20 breaths.

To Decrease Difficulty
- Roll your shoulders as well as your head.
- Continue to exhale until your mouth is clear of the water.
- Wear goggles.

7. Timing Drill on Pulling and Breathing

Repeat Drill 6, but this time emphasize the timing. Take your breath quickly while your breathing-side arm is *pulling*, not while it is recovering. The inhalation should be complete before the recovery begins. Exhale slowly during both pull and recovery of the opposite arm, so you are still exhaling as your mouth breaks water for the next inhalation. Allow your shoulders and body to roll to the side as you turn to breathe and to roll to the opposite side as you exhale.

Success Goal = 15 yards while pulling ___

Success Check
- Mouth open, grab quick breath ___
- Face back down while arm recovers ___
- Exhale slowly ___
- Pull all the way back ___

To Increase Difficulty
- Discard the float; kick.
- Work on timing.
- Change your breathing to the opposite side.

To Decrease Difficulty
- Wear goggles.
- Cut your distance to 10 yards.

8. One-Arm Pull and Breathing With Kickboard

Hold a kickboard with both hands and attach a deep leg float to your breathing-side ankle. Start by floating prone and exhaling, then hold the kickboard with the non-breathing-side hand as you pull and breathe on your breathing side. Replace your pulling hand on the board and hold the float position while exhaling. Continue to pull only with the breathing-side arm while inhaling and to float motionless while exhaling. To facilitate breathing, roll your shoulders while pulling. Keep your ear under water.

Success Goal = 10 successful pulls and breaths ___

Success Check
• Pull long and full ___
• Quick breath during pull, not during recovery ___
• Face down quickly after inhaling ___
• Motionless float while exhaling slowly ___

To Increase Difficulty
• Discard the kickboard; float free.
• Roll onto your side and recover the pulling arm *over* the water, back to the kickboard.
• Discard the float; kick.

To Decrease Difficulty
• Roll farther during the pull.
• Reduce the goal number of successful breaths.

9. Pulling and Breathing Without Support

Without a leg-support float, allow your legs to move as they wish as you pull and breathe. Begin with an exhalation and pull of the non-breathing arm. If your feet sink, be sure that your head is down during exhalation and that your ear is on the water during inhalation. Be sure to eliminate any downward push on the water with your hands. The pull must be horizontal under your body. Push the water backward under the centerline of your body.

Success Goal = 15 yards ___

Success Check
• Keep your head low in the water ___
• Pull and push horizontally, not downward ___
• Roll to the side to breathe ___

To Increase Difficulty
• Change your breathing to the opposite side.
• Keep your legs together; do not kick.

To Decrease Difficulty
• Do not try to hold your feet still.
• Roll your head, shoulders, and body to breathe.
• Cut your goal to 10 yards.
• Wear goggles.

10. Pull, Kick, and Breathe Without Support

Start from a prone-float position. Begin to kick gently. After four or five kicks, begin to pull and breathe to the side. Start with an exhalation and a pull of the non-breathing arm. Continue to kick while pulling and breathing. If you lose your coordination, stop and start over. Keep the kick small; do not concentrate on it. Breathe on *every* pull of the breathing-side arm.

Success Goal = 15 yards ____

Success Check
• Begin to add a small gentle kick ____
• Exhale and pull with non-breathing-side arm ____
• Roll head, shoulders, and body; breathe on the pull of the breathing-side arm ____

To Increase Difficulty
• Breathe on the opposite side.
• Breathe every third arm pull on alternate sides.

To Decrease Difficulty
• Wear goggles.
• Roll onto your side during the breathing-side pull.
• Decrease your goal to 10 yards.

11. Shallow-Water Kick, Pull, Breathe, and Turn Without Support

Repeat Drill 10. After a few strokes, reach and pull to one side to effect a turn. Swim across the pool, make a wide turn, and return. Continue to breathe on every breathing-side pull while turning.

Success Goal = 2 round trips without stopping ____

Success Check
• Take long easy pulls ____
• Kick gently ____
• Keep head low, pull level ____
• Look and reach in direction of turn ____

To Increase Difficulty
• On the second round trip, turn in the opposite direction.
• Breathe on the opposite side.

To Decrease Difficulty
• Start with one round trip.
• Wear a float belt.
• Wear goggles.

12. Deep-Water Pull, Kick, Breathe, and Turn

CAUTION: *Do not attempt this drill without a safety float belt unless you have an instructor or trained lifeguard with you.*

Have an expert swimmer with you and *wear a safety float belt* as you begin to swim and breathe at the shallow end of the pool. Swim to the deep end of the pool, make a wide turn, and return to the shallow end. Breathe on every breathing-side pull.

Success Goal = 2 pool lengths or 50 yards ___

Success Check
• Take long, full pulls ___
• Keep your head low ___
• Kick gently throughout ___
• Breathe on every breathing-side arm pull ___

To Increase Difficulty
• Breathe on alternate sides (every third pull).
• Swim a full circle in deep water before starting back to the shallow end.

To Decrease Difficulty
• Wear a large safety float belt.
• Wear goggles.
• Swim into deep water and back, but do not swim the whole pool length.

BREATHING SUCCESS SUMMARY

If you have reached the success goals in each of the drills in this step, you have mastered the most difficult skill in swimming. The steps to success in swimming become less steep at this point, and each skill becomes easier. Before you move ahead, however, it would be wise to have a skilled swimmer or someone who has a trained eye for swimming detail evaluate your pulling and breathing skills using the items in Figure 6.3. Perhaps you would profit from more practice on a few of these skills before moving on.

You will now be focusing on increasing the efficiency of the propulsive motions by learning some of the intermediate-level stroke packages.

STEP 7

TURNOVER AND GLIDE: BALANCED ON THE EDGE

The astronauts discovered that in a weightless state they could take and maintain any position they wished. They learned to control their body positions in space by practicing in tanks of water. Immersion in water is about as near to a weightless state as most of us will ever get. In water we can balance our bodies to maintain any position we desire. Swimmers achieve and maintain body position by balancing their bodies around the center of buoyancy: the lungs. In this chapter you will learn how to control your body position through balance. Knowing how to achieve and maintain balance will give you the freedom and confidence to be a better swimmer.

Turning Over

Breathing is much easier if your body is turned partly to the side to get your mouth above water. The ability to control that turn helps you breathe correctly. You can also roll completely onto your back.

Why Is Turning Over Important?

Swimming on your back allows you to keep your face clear of the water. On occasion, especially when learning, you may inhale at the wrong time in a prone position and inhale some water. If you were in deep water when this happened, the ability to roll over onto your back to rest, cough, and keep your face clear of the water for a few moments could save your life. In addition, the ability to roll your body at will is a necessary progression from the basic arm stroke to the overarm stroke used in the crawl. Later you will see how turning onto your side greatly facilitates breathing during an overhand arm recovery.

How to Turn Over

Use the deep-float leg support for this skill. Put your breathing-side foot in the loop of the deep-float leg support. Pull and breathe to the side. Do not try to kick, but keep your feet close together. On the third pull of the breathing-side arm, turn your head farther than usual, take a big breath, and raise your chin. Pull past your thigh and move the whole arm back behind you (see Figure 7.1a). Let the arm guide you over onto your back. *Arch your back.* It is very important to arch your back and lift your hips into the back-float position (see Figure 7.1b). Hold a big breath until you are steady in a back-float with arms above shoulder height (see Figure 7.1c). Relax. Breathe. Scull if you need support. Take a breath. Bring the breathing-side arm down to your hips and on across your body. Turn your head *away* from the breathing side, drop your chin, and bend slightly forward at the hips. Your body will roll into a face-down position (see Figure 7.1d) Continue pulling and breathing.

FIGURE
7.1

TURNING OVER

Preparation

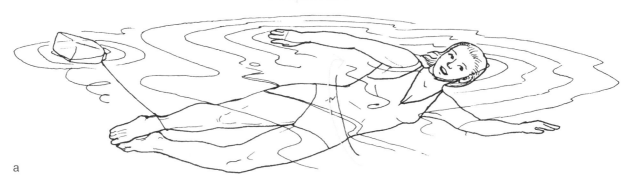

a

1. Pull and breathe three strokes with deep-float leg support ___

Execution

b

2. Pull breathing-side arm past thigh; reach behind body ___
3. Hold big breath, arch, chin up, roll onto back ___

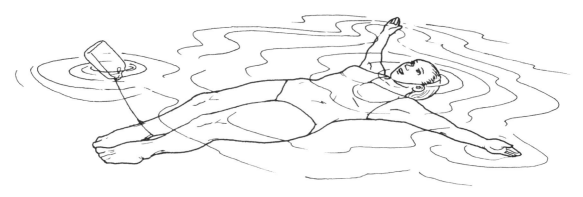

c

4. Both arms up beyond shoulders; relax ___

Recovery

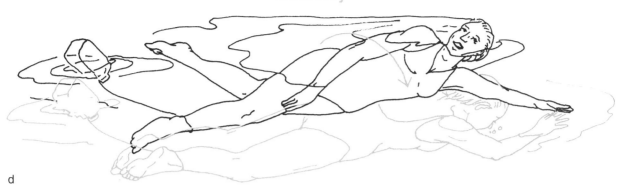

d

5. Bring breathing-side arm down past thigh, across body ____
6. Turn head away from breathing-side arm, roll forward into prone position ____
7. Continue pulling ____

Side Glide

The ability to turn over is an exercise in body positioning and balance. Now you are going to refine that technique of body positioning by maintaining a delicate balanced position on your side.

Why Is the Side Glide Important?

We are fortunate in being able to assume virtually any position we wish while floating in the water. We do it by balancing our weight around the center of buoyancy in the body: the lungs. Being able to feel and adjust the balance of your body to attain any desired position is a vital part of water technique. The side glide would be worth learning just for its contribution to our overall safety in the water through increased body balance and position awareness, but it is important for another reason also. This specific position is the basis for the most powerful swimming stroke we know: the sidestroke. It is also the position from which the overhand arm motion must be made for the crawl stroke if we wish to swim smoothly and expertly and breathe without stress.

The key to the side glide is balance. If you arch your back, you will float on your back. If you bend forward at the hips, you will float face down. If your body is stretched, subtle variations in the bend of the hips or arch of the back will allow you to maintain a side-float position.

How to Execute the Side Glide

While swimming in the prone position, pull through with the breathing-side arm, and turn your body onto the side to breathe (see Figure 7.2a). Stop with the breathing arm resting on your side and the opposite arm stretched forward (see Figure 7.2b). Keep your ear pressed tightly to the forward arm and hold the side glide for about 3 to 4 seconds. Return to the prone position, and resume stroking (see Figure 7.2c). Pull with the opposite arm while rolling to the opposite side. Take a breath and hold a side glide on that side for 3 to 4 seconds also. Continue to stop and glide on each side.

FIGURE
7.2

SIDE GLIDE

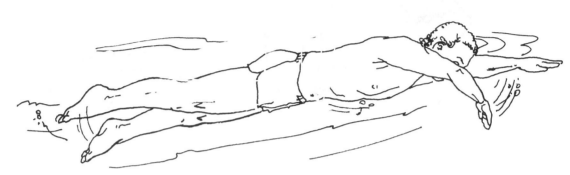

a

1. Kick while pulling ___
2. Face downward ___
3. Pull; roll to breathing side ___

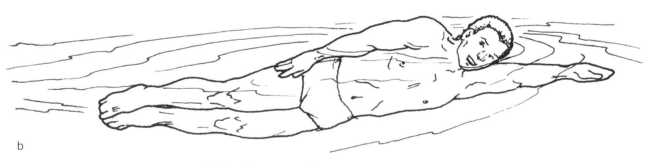

b

4. Breathe; stop with hand on thigh ___
5. Forward arm stretched; ear on arm ___
6. Hold 4 seconds ___

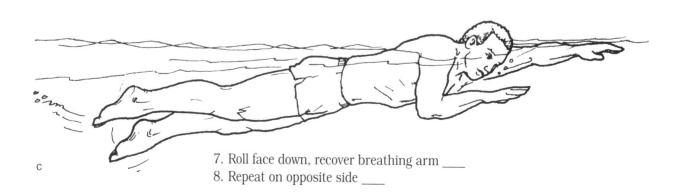

c

7. Roll face down, recover breathing arm ___
8. Repeat on opposite side ___

TURNOVER AND GLIDE SUCCESS STOPPERS

Turning over is easy, but gliding on your side is tricky. Errors are inevitable in the beginning. If you have trouble with either, try the corrections listed.

ERROR	CORRECTION
Turnover	
1. You fail to roll over onto your back.	1. Raise your chin. Arch your back. Reach your arm behind you.
2. You sink when on your back.	2. Take a bigger breath; scull for support.
3. Water gets into your nose.	3. Exhale quickly through your nose as you roll; take a big breath.
4. You have trouble starting your roll back to prone position.	4. Look and reach in the direction you want to go; bend forward at the hips.
5. Roll toward stomach is too slow.	5. Step forward with your top leg.
Side Glide	
1. You roll face down.	1. Arch your back slightly.
2. You roll onto your back.	2. Bend slightly forward at hips.
3. Your body sinks.	3. Take a deeper breath; keep rear arm under water against side.
4. Your feet sink.	4. Hold the glide only until forward motion slows; keep your ear pressed against lower arm.
5. Your head sinks.	5. Keep forward arm under your head.
6. You breathe water.	6. Roll slightly more onto your back; keep your ear pressed against the lower arm.

DRILLS

1. Turnover

In shallow water, use the deep-float leg support for this skill (see Figure 7.1). Put your breathing-side foot in the loop of the deep-float leg support. Pull and breathe to the side. Do not try to kick, but keep your feet close together. On the third pull of the breathing-side arm, turn your head farther than usual, take a big breath, and raise your chin. Pull past your thigh and move the whole arm back behind you. Let the arm guide you over onto your back. *Arch your back.* It is very important to arch your back and lift your hips into the back-float position. Hold a big breath until you are steady in a back float with your arms above shoulder height. Relax. Breathe. Scull if you need support. Take a big breath. Bring the breathing-side arm down to your hips and on across your body. Turn your head *away* from the breathing side, drop your chin, and bend slightly forward at the hips. Your body will roll into a face-down position. Continue pulling and breathing.

Success Goal = 8 front-to-back and
back-to-front turns ___

Success Check
• Pull and roll, move arm behind you ___
• Take a big breath, arch your back ___
• Float, breathe, scull if you need to ___
• Turn face away, roll, bring top arm to front ___
• Bend hips, face down, pull and breathe ___

To Increase Difficulty
• Eliminate the leg float.
• Swim three strokes in basic back stroke before turning to prone position.

To Decrease Difficulty
• Step back with your top leg as your arm moves behind you.
• Wear a float belt.

2. Turning Over Without Support

Float; pull and kick without support. Turn over front to back and back to front. Keep your feet close together while turning over. Use a support kick while on your back.

Success Goal = 5 front-to-back and
back-to-front turns ___

Success Check
• Pull, roll, reach back ___
• Take a big breath, arch ___
• Kick, breathe ___
• Look away, roll, top arm to front ___

To Increase Difficulty
• While on your back, make a U-turn before rolling to prone position.

To Decrease Difficulty
• Wear a float belt.
• Do three turns each way.

3. Front-to-Back Deep-Water Turnover

Start in shallow water and swim into deep water in a prone position. Make sure to *wear a safety float belt* and have an expert swimmer with you. Make a wide turn and start back; then turn over onto your back and swim into shallow water using the back arm stroke and kick. *CAUTION: Do not try this drill without a safety float belt unless you have a trained lifeguard with you.*

Success Goal = 3 round trips ____

Success Check

- Wear a float belt ____
- Breathe every breathing-side arm stroke while swimming prone ____
- Make a U-turn before turning over ____
- Arch, chin up, when rolling over ____
- Basic back stroke and propulsion kick on back ____

To Increase Difficulty

- Swim all the way to the deep end before turning.
- On one round trip, roll over onto your back before making the U-turn.
- *Have a trained lifeguard with you* and swim without the safety belt.

To Decrease Difficulty

- Have the swimmer or lifeguard stay with you.
- Make the U-turn immediately after entering deep water.
- Wear goggles.

4. Back-to-Front Deep-Water Turnover

Start in shallow water on your back. *Wear a safety float belt* and have a good swimmer with you. Swim into deep water, make a wide U-turn; roll over into a prone position and swim back to shallow water. *CAUTION: If you swim without a safety float belt, make sure a trained lifeguard is present.*

Success Goal = 3 round trips ____

Success Check

- Wear a safety float belt ____
- Use basic back stroke and propulsion kick ____
- Make your turn wide ____
- Take a big breath before rolling over ____
- Breathe every breathing-side arm stroke while swimming prone ____

To Increase Difficulty

- On one round trip, turn over before making the U-turn.
- *Have a trained lifeguard with you* and eliminate the safety float.

To Decrease Difficulty

- Make your U-turn immediately after entering deep water.
- Wear goggles.
- Stay near the pool edge.

Wear a safety float belt and have a good swimmer with you. Start at the shallow end of the pool and swim prone into deep water to the other end of the pool (or about 25 yards) Then make a wide turn and start back to the shallow end. After three strokes, turn over onto your back and rest as nearly motionless as possible for 1 full minute. Turn over into a prone position again and swim back to the shallow end. *CAUTION: Do not try this drill without a safety float belt or a trained lifeguard watching you.*

Success Goal = 2 round trips of 50 yards ___

Success Check
• Swim slowly, breathe every breathing-side stroke ___
• Arch your back, chin and arms up for float ___
• Take a big breath before rolling into prone position ___

To Increase Difficulty
• Do the U-turn while floating, with as little motion as possible.
• *Have a trained lifeguard watching you* and eliminate the safety float belt.

To Decrease Difficulty
• Cut the distance to 40 yards.
• Wear goggles.
• Rest twice—on the way out and on the way back.

With a trained lifeguard watching you, swim continuously up and down the pool. Turn over onto your back and swim part way. Stop and float to rest as often and for as long as you wish.

Success Goal = 100 yards ___

Success Check
• Swim slowly, breathing rhythmically ___
• Make your turnovers smoothly with deep breaths on each ___
• Make wide turns ___

To Increase Difficulty
• Swim as far as you can, up to 200 yards.
• Swim the first 50 yards on your back and the second 50 yards in prone position.

To Decrease Difficulty
• Wear a safety float belt.
• Have the lifeguard swim with you.
• Wear goggles.

7. Front-to-Back Turnover Through the Vertical

In shoulder-deep water swim in prone position. Take a breath, hold it, and stop swimming. Press down with both hands on the water in front of you, raise your head, and tuck your knees under you; this will cause your feet to drop down to a vertical position. When your feet are under you, arch your back, put your head back, scull, and step up to the surface with a back-support kick. You should make an easy transition *through the vertical* to a back-swimming position.

a

b

Success Goal = 5 front-to-back transitions ___

Success Check
• Take a breath, stop with both arms in front ___
• Tuck your knees as you press down and back ___
• Head back, scull, and step up ___

To Increase Difficulty
• Stop and hold in the vertical position for several seconds while sculling.
• Don't tuck your knees.

To Decrease Difficulty
• Wear a float belt.
• Wear a nose clip.

8. Back-to-Front Turnover Through the Vertical

In shoulder-deep water, swim on your back. Take a deep breath and stop swimming. Sit up and tuck your feet under you. Put your face down and arms forward, as you extend one foot up behind you as far as you can reach and press down on the water with the top of your foot. Then step up behind you with the other foot and press down again. Reach out in front and start your arm pull. You should make the back-to-front transition *through the vertical* position.

a

b

Success Goal = 5 back-to-front vertical transitions ___

Success Check
• Take a deep breath, tuck your knees ___
• Reach arms forward, face down ___
• Step up behind and press with your foot ___
• Step up behind and press with your other foot, start to pull forward with your arms ___

To Increase Difficulty
• Keep your arms out to the side and do the drill entirely with your feet.
• Keep your knees tucked up, put your face in the water, and extend your arms forward. Hold that position until you are floating face down, then simply extend your legs to the rear and start swimming.

To Decrease Difficulty
• Wear a float belt.
• Wear goggles.

9. Side Glide From Push-Off With Leg Support

Use the deep-float leg support on your breathing-side ankle. Hold the edge of the pool with your breathing-side hand. Turn sideways to the pool wall, extend the opposite arm out toward open water, put both feet against the wall near the top, and lay your ear on the forward arm.

Take a deep breath and push off from the wall on your side, extending and streamlining your body. Keep the trailing arm against your side, and glide as long as possible. Control your balance on the side by bending very slightly at the hips as needed. If you tend to roll face down, arch your back just a little. If you tend to roll face up, bend very slightly forward at the hips. Breathe deeply and hold each breath.

Success Goal = 20 seconds ____

Success Check
• Push steadily to full extension ____
• Turn head just enough to keep mouth clear ____
• Concentrate on balance through hip bend or extension ____
• Keep your lungs full ____

To Increase Difficulty
• Try for 30 seconds.
• Eliminate the leg support.

To Decrease Difficulty
• Hold the side position for only 10 seconds.
• Experiment to find how little hip bend or extension corrects the tendency to roll.
• Hold the side position, but turn your face down so it is just under water. Hold your breath.
• Wear a mask and snorkel with the snorkel on the top side of the mask. Be careful to keep the end of the snorkel out of the water.

10. Opposite Side Glide

Attach the deep-float leg support to the other leg and repeat Drill 9 on the opposite side, but keep your face turned down into the water. Do not lift your head. Hold your breath.

Success Goal = 20 seconds in side position ____

Success Check
• Push off steadily on your side, face turned down ____
• Body straight and streamlined with tiny hip bend or arching to control balance ____
• Lungs full, hold your breath ____

To Increase Difficulty
• Try for 30 seconds of balanced side float.
• Eliminate the leg float.

To Decrease Difficulty
• Hold balanced position for only 10 seconds.
• Wear a mask and snorkel with the snorkel attached to the top side of the mask.

11. Side Glide Without Support

Push off the side in side-glide position with no float support. Glide only as long as your feet remain near the surface. Concentrate on balancing in the side position. Glide on each side. Keep your face in the water if you prefer.

Success Goal = 4 glides on each side without rolling ___

Success Check
• Solid but steady push-off ___
• Hold a big breath ___
• Balance on your side by arching or bending ___

To Increase Difficulty
• Try for 10-second side floats.
• Glide for distance. See how far you can go before your feet sink.

To Decrease Difficulty
• Wear a mask and snorkel (snorkel on the top).

12. Pull and Side Glide, Breathing Side Only

Attach the deep-float leg support to your ankle on your breathing side. Start pulling and breathing in the prone position. Beginning with the third stroke of the breathing arm, pull the arm to your side, roll into a side glide, and take a breath. Keep your ear in the water. Hold the glide for 4 seconds, then resume stroking. Stop in the side glide position for 4 seconds *every time* your breathing arm pulls.

Success Goal = 5 consecutive, breathing-side glides ___

Success Check
• Pull arm to your side as you roll into side glide ___
• Slow count to four, then resume stroking ___
• Side glide, count four, every breathing-arm cycle ___

To Increase Difficulty
• Eliminate the leg float. Kick as you pull, but stop kicking during the glide.
• Make 10 consecutive, breathing-side glides.

To Decrease Difficulty
• Take a *big* breath for each glide.
• Finish each pull and recovery before starting the next.
• Exhale completely on the opposite arm pull.

13. Pull and Side Glide, Nonbreathing Side Only

Attach the deep float to the ankle of your nonbreathing side. Change your breathing pattern to breathe on the opposite side for this drill. The side glide will give you plenty of time to get a breath, even though it seems awkward. You will need a little practice to get used to a new breathing pattern. Pull and stop 4 seconds to breathe in a side glide each time the new breathing-side arm reaches your hip.

Success Goal = 5 consecutive, 4-second glides ____

Success Check
- Roll as you pull ____
- Take a breath and hold the glide 4 seconds ____
- Resume pulling, glide on each new breathing-side pull ____

To Increase Difficulty
- Execute the drill without the leg float. Kick while you pull, but stop kicking while you glide.
- Make 10 consecutive side glides.

To Decrease Difficulty
- Keep your body straight during the glide.
- Take a *big* breath on the glide.
- Exhale completely on the opposite side pull.

14. Pull and Side Glide Without Support Float

Repeat Drills 12 and 13 without the leg support. Kick gently for leg support while stroking, but stop all motion for the glide. Cut the glide time to 3 seconds.

Success Goal = 5 consecutive, 3-second glides on each side ____

Success Check
- Take big breaths on each glide ____
- Keep head on the water ____
- Keep arm on top hip ____

To Increase Difficulty
- Make 10 consecutive glides on each side.

To Decrease Difficulty
- Wear a mask and snorkel. Keep snorkel on the top side of the mask.

15. Glide With Every Arm Stroke

While swimming in a prone position, and using a small kick, pull into a side glide with *each* arm stroke. Hold each glide for only 2 seconds, but make a definite stop and glide with your top arm resting on your side. Breathe only on your usual breathing side. Turn your shoulders and body to a side-glide position on the opposite side, but keep your face turned into the water on that side. Stroke slowly and make each stroke full and deliberate. Adjust your breathing to the slower pace required.

Success Goal = 10 consecutive, alternate side glides ____

Success Check
- Pull and glide, pull and glide smoothly ____
- Long pulls; full recovery after each ____
- Breathe on one side only; hold your breath on the other side glide ____

To Increase Difficulty
- Make 20 consecutive, alternate side glides.
- Recover each arm *over* the water.

To Decrease Difficulty
- Wear a mask.
- Exhale and inhale on each arm stroke.

If you have completed the success goals for each of the drills in this step, you have mastered the necessary balance factors to achieve any body position you desire. You also have the skill to breathe on either side at will. An expert swimmer or instructor should check your skills, using the keys to success in Figure 7.1 and in Figure 7.2 to evaluate your accomplishments.

You are ready now to learn the most powerful stroke in swimming: the sidestroke.

STEP 8

SIDESTROKE: LIFEGUARD POWER STROKE

The sidestroke has a colorful history. In 1886 H. Kenworthy wrote in *A Treatise On The Utility Of Swimming*, "Until within the last few years it was generally supposed that Breast or Belly swimming was the swiftest process, but this opinion has proved fallacious. The side stroke is now universally acknowledged as the superior method and young swimmers would do well to practice it accordingly."[1]

Today we recognize the sidestroke not as the swiftest, but as the most powerful, swimming stroke. The sidestroke is the lifesaving stroke. A lifeguard attempting a rescue without equipment must carry the weight of a drowning victim and give up the use of one arm while swimming back to shore. The sidestroke is the stroke of choice when such power is needed. It employs a scissors kick to supply the power. This step is all about the scissors kick and the sidestroke.

Scissors Kick

Swimmers perform the scissors kick in the side-glide position. Because you already know the side-glide position you should have no trouble learning the scissors kick.

Why Is the Scissors Kick Important?

The scissors kick is important because of its power. It provides a longer glide and rest than any other kick and is easy to learn because it uses the forward-back motion that we use for walking. The scissors kick is the workhorse of all the kicks.

How to Execute a Scissors Kick

Hold a kickboard under one ear like a violin. Start in a side-glide position and bend at the knees and hips to bring both feet in a direct line toward your body (see Figure 8.1a). When your knees are fully bent (hips at 90 degrees), hook the top foot and step out forward as if to step up onto a high step. At the same time, point the toes of your lower foot and step back as far as you can, as if to lay your toes on top of a large step behind you (see Figure 8.1b) Now step forward *and back* as far as you can as the legs thrust and squeeze; straighten to full extension (see Figure 8.1c). Point the toes of both feet during the thrust. Finish with feet together and streamlined. Turn your toes in slightly so they catch on each other at the finish. G-l-i-d-e!

---

[1]Robertson, D.F. (1977). *The History and Development of Men's Intercollegiate Swimming in the United States from 1897 to 1970*. Unpublished doctoral dissertation, Ohio State University.

FIGURE
8.1

SCISSORS KICK

a

1. Side-glide position; kickboard under ear ___
2. Legs tucked, hips at 90 degrees ___
3. Feet in line with body ___

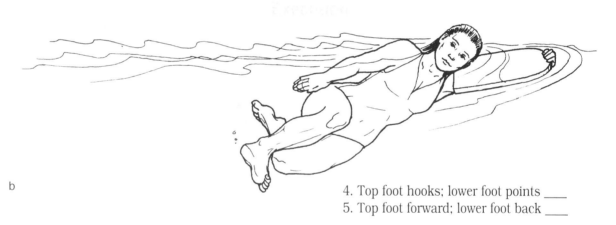

b

4. Top foot hooks; lower foot points ___
5. Top foot forward; lower foot back ___

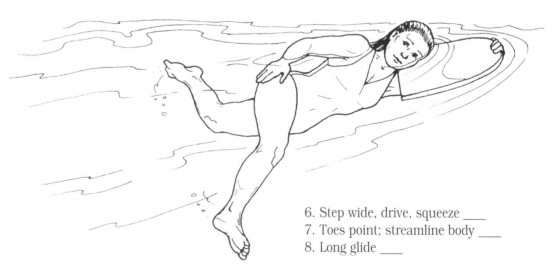

6. Step wide, drive, squeeze ___
7. Toes point; streamline body ___
8. Long glide ___

c

Sidestroke Arm Motion

The sidestroke arm motion is sometimes likened to lying on your side, picking apples, and putting them into a basket. Think of reaching over your head with one hand to pick an apple, then bringing the apple down to your chin. The other hand then takes the apple and carries it downward to your knee to put it in the basket. As the lower hand puts the apple in the basket, the upper hand is reaching for another apple. Substitute a good handful of water for the apple and you have the sidestroke arm motion.

The arms move in opposite directions in the sidestroke. The upper, rearward arm pushes simultaneously with the thrust of the kick, and the lower, forward arm pulls as the legs and other arm recover.

Why Is the Sidestroke Arm Motion Important?

The importance of the sidestroke arm motion derives from the importance of the stroke itself. It is not a powerful arm stroke, but it is essential to the most powerful stroke we know.

Only one arm pattern fits the sidestroke. It is unique in that it is the only arm pull that allows the use of one arm to carry something or someone while the other arm continues its pull.

How to Execute the Sidestroke Arm Motion

Use a deep-float leg float attached to your top leg in a side-glide position with one arm extended forward under your head and the other arm along your side. Flex the forward (lower) wrist to put your hand in position to pull back horizontally. Start the pull of the forward arm by bending your elbow and pulling back with your hand and forearm. Allow your hand and forearm to assume a horizontal position, elbow bent 90 degrees, as you begin to pull from the shoulder. Pull as though you were gathering an armful of water and pulling it in to your chest (see Figure 8.2a). When the forward elbow is pointing straight down, bring your hand up under your ear, and turn it palm up (see Figure 8.2b). Squeeze your elbow to your side; point your fingertips forward; and extend your arm, palm up, just under the surface to full extension (see Figure 8.2c). Turn the palm down as it reaches full extension. Glide until you are ready for the next stroke.

The upper, rearward arm moves in opposition to the forward arm. As the forward arm begins its pull, keep the elbow of your top arm close to your side. Bend it and bring that hand to your chin (see Figure 8.2b). Leave your palm down and slice your hand edgewise through the water as it moves. As the forward hand is turning palm up under your lower ear, bring your top arm forward to shoulder height; plunge your hand deep into the water in front of your face. Your top arm is now at shoulder height, your elbow is bent 90 degrees, and your fingers are pointing straight down to the bottom of the pool. As your forward arm extends to starting position, your top arm pushes water directly backward toward your feet with the forearm and hand. Continue to push with the top arm until it rests once again along your side. This final motion returns your body to a streamlined position for the glide.

FIGURE
8.2

SIDESTROKE ARM MOTION

Rearward (upper) arm does this   while   Forward (lower) arm does this

1. Straight, along side, relaxed ___
2. Elbow in, hand slices to chin ___
3. Arm at shoulder height; elbow bent 90 degrees ___
4. Hand points down, palm toward feet ___
5. Push water toward the feet, hand ends on thigh ___

1. Wrist flexes, fingers point down ___
2. Elbow bent 90 degrees during pull ___
3. Pull ends at shoulder ___
4. Palm up, under ear ___
5. Arm extends, hand turns palm down ___
6. G-l-i-d-e ___

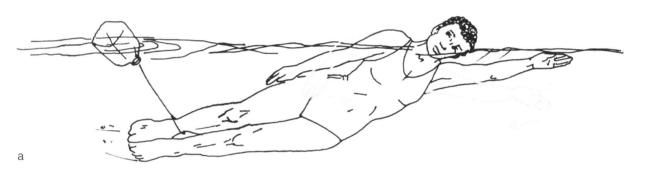

a

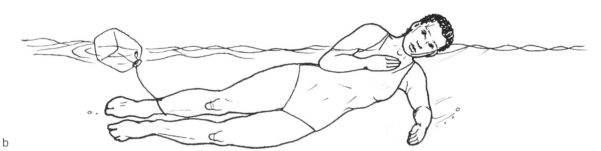

b

c

Sidestroke

The sidestroke is a kick-intensive stroke: Most of its power is derived from the kick. One arm aids the kick in propulsion, but the other arm simply compensates for the negative effect of the leg recovery.

Why Is the Sidestroke Important?

The sidestroke employs the scissors kick, which is so powerful that it does not need the added propulsion provided by the top arm. This means that one arm can be free to do other things. It is possible to carry or tow rather heavy objects or people simply by shortening the glide somewhat. If you choose to use both arms, this stroke allows you the longest glide,

or rest period, of any stroke. Also, your face is always above water so you may breathe at any time you wish. For swimming long distances the sidestroke is the most efficient stroke.

How to Swim the Sidestroke

From a side-glide position (see Figure 8.3a), pull with your forward arm as your legs and top arm recover (see Figure 8.3b). Thrust with the scissors kick and push backward with your top arm as your forward arm recovers (see Figure 8.3c). The kick coincides with the forward thrust of the forward arm, ending the stroke with power and in the streamlined position for a long glide (see Figure 8.3d). It seems almost as if your top hand and your legs were tied together, because they move in the same direction at the same time.

FIGURE 8.3   KEYS TO SUCCESS

SIDESTROKE
Preparation

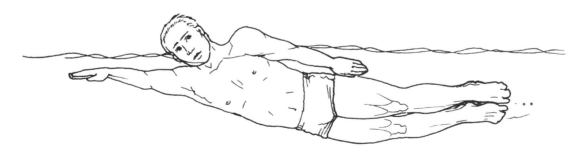

a

1. Easy, relaxed, side glide ___

SIDESTROKE

Forward arm does this	*while*	**Legs and top arm do this**
1. Pull to shoulder; inhale; palm under ear ___		1. Draw knees up; slice top hand to chin ___
2. Forward elbow in; fingers point forward ___		2. Feet step out; hand digs in ___
3. Forward arm extends; palm down ___		3. Strong leg kick; top arm push ___
		4. Long glide; exhale ___

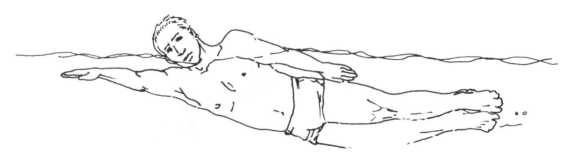

b

c

d

SIDESTROKE SUCCESS STOPPERS

Errors in the scissors kick, sidestroke arm motion, and sidestroke should be caught early and corrected. Use these common errors and corrections to perfect your technique.

ERROR	CORRECTION
Scissors Kick	
1. Your feet are forward of your body in tuck position.	1. Bend 90 degrees at your hips; bend knees more.
2. Your lower thigh still points forward after stepping out.	2. Step back farther with your lower leg.
3. Stepping out rolls you onto your stomach.	3. Consciously roll your hips back.
4. Your legs thrust straight back.	4. Step *out*, around, and thrust.
5. Your feet pass each other.	5. Turn your feet inward to cross and catch.
Sidestroke Arm Motion	
1. Your forward arm pulls out in front of you.	1. Pull *down* with your elbow bent.
2. Your forward arm pulls too far.	2. Don't pull past your shoulder. Bring your hand up to your ear.
3. You lift your head while pulling your lower arm.	3. Keep your ear under water.
4. You push water forward on the lower arm extension.	4. Keep your wrist straight, hand flat, and fingertips forward.
5. You are pushing water on the top arm recovery.	5. Keep your palm flat and wrist straight. Slice your hand through the water.
6. Your top arm is out of the water.	6. Bend your top elbow, dig your hand deep to push.
7. Your top hand comes too far forward.	7. Dig your hand in at your chin.
Sidestroke	
1. Your armpull-kick coordination is wrong.	1. The top arm should push with the kick; the lower arm should pull while your legs recover.
2. You move diagonally or in a long curve.	2. Step back farther with your lower leg.

DRILLS

1. Scissors Kick Land Drill

Lie on your side on a mat, one arm stretched forward under your ear, the other along your side. Bring your knees up, but keep your feet back in line with your body. Check the position of your feet. Point the toes of the lower foot and hook the upper foot at the ankle. Step out forward with the top foot and back with the bottom leg in as big a step as possible without rolling the hips forward. Stop and check to see if the lower leg is as far back as it will go (lower thigh straight with body). Then carefully move the feet *out*, around, and then down together in a circular motion. Streamline the legs and toes as for a glide.

a

b

c

Success Goal = 10 or more correct kicks ___

Success Check
- Knees bent, thighs at 90 degrees ___
- Feet in direct line with body ___
- Point lower toes, hook upper foot ___
- Step forward and back ___
- Feet *out*, around, and then down ___
- Legs straight, toes pointed, streamline ___

To Increase Difficulty
- Gradually increase speed and smoothness.
- Ask a critical expert to correct you.

To Decrease Difficulty
- Move slowly, stop and check each position.
- Place top hand on mat for balance.

2. Scissors Kick Bracket Drill

In shallow water at the side of the pool, turn your side to the wall. Lay your cheek on the water with your head toward the wall. Grasp the pool edge with your top hand. Place the bottom hand against the pool wall about 18 inches down with your palm against the wall and fingertips pointing down (bracket position). The lower hand must be directly under the top hand (see Figure a). Now pull slightly with the top hand and push slightly with the bottom hand to bring your feet off the bottom in a side-float position. If your body moves to the side, move the bottom hand slightly in the same direction until you can hold the side position comfortably. Keep your ear under water. Recover your legs slowly, as in the land drill; hook the top foot, point the lower foot, step out *slowly* (top foot forward, bottom foot back); then drive out, around, and down with vigor (see Figure b). Stop in the glide position. Do not let your feet pass.

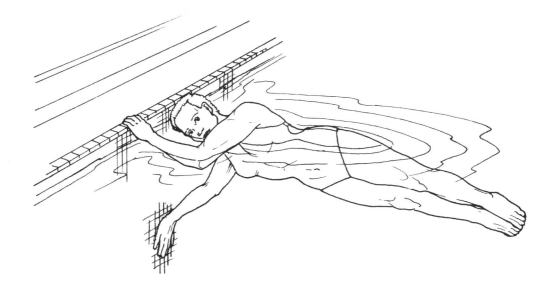

a

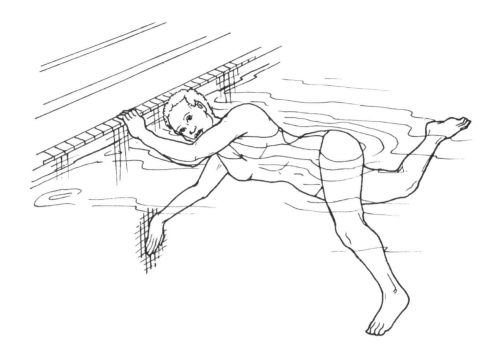

b

Success Goal = 30 bracket drill
kicks ___

Success Check
• Draw knees up to 90 degrees, feet in line with but-tocks ___
• Keep hips vertical, step out wide ___
• Draw up slowly, kick with vigor ___
• Streamlined finish; pointed toes ___

To Increase Difficulty
• Allow your elbows to bend slightly as the kick drives you into the wall.

To Decrease Difficulty
• Find a steady, balanced bracket position before starting the drill.
• Start in slow motion, gradually increase vigor.

Take a side-float position: lower arm extended under your head, upper arm along your side. Hold a kickboard lengthwise under the top arm, fairly close to the hip. Use the scissors kick across the pool.

Success Goal = 15 yards ___

Success Check
• Step *way* back, keep hips vertical ___
• Hold streamlined position for long glide ___

To Increase Difficulty
• Scull with your lower arm while you draw your knees up.
• Try kicking on the other side.

To Decrease Difficulty
• Move the kickboard slightly forward or back to help maintain your balance.
• Decrease the expected distance.
• Use a float belt instead of a kickboard.

4. Distance per Scissors Kick

Assume a side-glide position. Hold a kickboard lengthwise in your forward arm under your head, like a violin. Keep your ear pressed tightly to the board. Grasp the lower corner of the kickboard with the fingertips of your other hand. Push off the bottom into a side glide and begin the scissors kick. Make the kick as wide as you can and try for distance on the glide. Remember to balance on the side for the glide by bending slightly at the hips to prevent rolling onto your back. Arch slightly to prevent rolling onto your stomach. Kick across the pool.

Success Goal = 10 feet per kick (average) ____

Success Check
• Draw your knees up slowly ____
• Step out wide and thrust back hard ____
• Streamline, coast in long, balanced side glide ____

To Increase Difficulty
• Try the drill without a kickboard.
• Hold the kickboard at arm's length.

To Decrease Difficulty
• Use a float belt instead of a kickboard.
• Do not ride your glide to a complete stop.

5. Scissors Kick for Distance

Using a kickboard either under your ear or on your top hip, kick across the pool. Turn immediately, push off, and kick back again. Continue without stopping to rest on the turns until you have completed four pool widths (about 180 feet). Stay in shallow water.

Success Goal = 4 pool widths ____

Success Check
• Maintain an average of 10 feet per kick ____
• Streamline your body for a long glide ____
• Step wide, kick hard ____

To Increase Difficulty
• Eliminate the kickboard; use your hands for balance.

To Decrease Difficulty
• Inhale quickly on the kick; exhale slowly during the glide.
• Cut the goal distance to three pool widths (about 135 feet).

Hold the kickboard like a violin, but place your other hand on the front of the thigh of the top leg. As your legs recover for the scissors kick, allow the top hand to remain on the front of the thigh, elbow bending as necessary. During the thrust of the legs, push with the hand on the front of the thigh as if to help the leg push against the water. This is the first step in a progression to coordinate the sidestroke arm motion with the scissors kick.

Success Goal = 40 kicks with hand push ___

Success Check
- Recover your legs slowly ___
- Step way back with the bottom foot ___
- Press on your thigh with the top hand, and drive hard with the kick ___
- Streamline and glide ___

To Increase Difficulty
- Eliminate support; use your forward hand to scull for balance.
- Hold your top hand about 6 inches from your thigh; press on the water, not your leg.

To Decrease Difficulty
- Hold the kickboard at arm's length in front.
- Use a float belt instead of a kickboard.

Attach the deep-float leg support to one ankle and assume a side-glide position. Hold a kickboard under your upper arm; keep it fairly close to your armpit to support your upper body. Keep your ear on the water.

Flex the forward (lower) wrist to put your hand in position to pull back horizontally. Start the pull of the forward arm by bending your elbow and pulling back with your hand and forearm. Allow your hand and forearm to assume a horizontal position, elbow bent 90 degrees, as you begin to pull from the shoulder. Pull as though you were gathering an armful of water and pulling it in to your chest. When the forward elbow is pointing straight down, bring your hand up under your ear and turn it palm up. Squeeze your elbow to your side, point your fingertips forward, and extend the arm (palm up) just under the surface to full extension. Turn the palm down as it reaches full extension. Hold the glide position for a moment; then repeat the pull.

Pull in very slow motion as you float, so you can study the arm motion. Do not try for propulsion or distance at first. As you become accustomed to the motion, make the pull rather quickly and "sneak" the hand forward again, slowly, with the least possible resistance. Stop in the glide position, but do not expect to glide very far. Inhale as you pull; exhale as you glide (review Figure 8.2)

Success Goal = 40 pulls with breathing ___

Success Check
- Pull only to shoulder level ___
- Bring your hand to your ear, palm up ___
- Shoot your hand forward to full extension, turning the palm down ___

To Increase Difficulty
- Discard the kickboard and scull with the top hand.
- Turn over and try the pull with the other arm.

To Decrease Difficulty
- Move the kickboard forward or back for balance.
- Wear a float belt instead of using a kickboard.

8. Sidestroke Upper Arm Push With Support

Using the deep-float leg support, hold a kickboard under your ear like a violin in a side-float position. Start the motion by recovering the upper hand from its position on your thigh. Keep your hand flat on the water and your wrist straight. Leave your elbow close to your side as it bends, bringing your hand to your chin. As you dig downward into the water with your hand, allow your elbow to move forward until it is straight out in front of your shoulder. Keep a 90-degree bend in the elbow, with your fingertips pointing directly to the bottom of the pool. Now push water toward your feet with the forearm and hand until your arm is straight and resting on your thigh again. Inhale on the recovery; exhale on the glide (review Figure 8.2, p.80).

Success Goal = 40 upper arm thrusts with breathing and glide ____

Success Check
• Slice the flat palm edgewise through the water to your chin ____
• Bring elbow up to shoulder height, bent 90 degrees, hand and forearm pointing down ____
• Push with hand and forearm toward feet to full extension ____

To Increase Difficulty
• Discard the kickboard; scull with your forward hand.
• Try the drill on your other side.
• Pull with the forward arm while recovering your top arm.

To Decrease Difficulty
• Hold the board at arm's length in front.
• Wear a float belt instead of using a kickboard.

9. Coordinated Sidestroke Arm Pull, Feet Supported

Use the deep-leg support float, but no kickboard. Start in side-glide position. Pull with the forward arm as the top arm recovers and push with the top arm as the forward arm recovers. Move as though you were gathering an armful of water ahead of you and bringing it back to your chest. Then transfer the same water to your other hand to push it on toward your feet. As you begin to use both arms efficiently, you will get some forward motion. Do not expect a lot of propulsion, but ride each glide as far as you can (review Figure 8.2)

Success Goal = 45 feet ____

Success Check
• Move your arms in opposition to each other ____
• Slice hands through water on recovery to minimize resistance to forward motion ____
• Concentrate on quick pull of forward arm and solid push of top arm ____

To Increase Difficulty
• Concentrate on eliminating negative water-pushing by using flat hands positions.
• Increase your goal to 25 yards.

To Decrease Difficulty
• Wear a float belt.
• Start in very slow motion and gradually work toward normal stroke speed.

Hold a kickboard at arm's length with your forward hand. Lay your top hand on the front of the thigh of your top leg. Kick, using the scissors kick. Allow your elbow to bend as you recover your legs, but keep your hand on your leg. During the thrust of the kick, push on your thigh with your hand, as if to help it kick. After the third or fourth kick, gradually remove your hand from your thigh, but continue to make the same movement pattern with your hand 3 to 5 inches forward of your thigh.

Keep the same hand–leg coordination, but move your hand farther forward on each stroke until your hand is slicing to your chin and digging in to push on the water in correct sidestroke motion.

Success Goal = 45 feet ___

Success Check
- Let your hand ride on your leg for two kicks ___
- Push on your leg during extension for two kicks ___
- Move your hand forward of your leg so it pushes its own water for two kicks ___
- Move your hand forward to your chin and push water back simultaneously with the kick ___

To Increase Difficulty
- Discard the kickboard and scull with the forward arm.
- Pull with your forward arm while your legs recover.

To Decrease Difficulty
- Wear a float belt.
- Shorten the goal distance to 30 feet.

In sidestroke position hold a kickboard under your top arm near your top hip. From a glide position, pull with the forward arm and recover the legs for a scissors kick. Stop momentarily when your feet are ready to step out and your hand is under your ear. Check that everything is ready for a simultaneous leg thrust and arm extension to glide position. Then kick and reach into a long glide. Continue to hesitate at this coordination checkpoint for a few strokes; then eliminate the hesitation and swim the stroke smoothly with a long glide.

Success Goal = 40 pulls done smoothly and coordinated ___

Success Check
- Pull with forward arm while bringing knees up and stepping out ___
- Stop, check position, drive legs back and hand forward, glide ___
- Continue; eliminate check position ___

To Increase Difficulty
- Use no flotation; rest your top hand on your thigh and push your top leg while kicking.

To Decrease Difficulty
- Use a float belt instead of a kickboard; scull with top hand for balance.

12. Fully Coordinated Sidestroke

Push off from the side and swim a fully coordinated sidestroke across the shallow end of the pool. Turn and push off; swim back again. Continue to swim widths; concentrate on timing, smoothness, and distance per stroke.

Success Goal = 4 pool widths or 60 yards ___

Success Check
- Forward arm pulls while legs and top arm recover ___
- Forward arm extends while legs and top arm drive ___
- Glide at least one body length, ear on water ___
- Inhale on forward arm pull; exhale on glide ___

To Increase Difficulty
- Stretch and hold for a longer glide.
- Continue to swim for 100 yards.

To Decrease Difficulty
- Keep your ear underwater.
- Take a big breath on the forward arm pull, hold it during the kick, and exhale on the glide.

13. Side Stroke, Distance per Stroke

Push off the side wall and swim a fully coordinated sidestroke across the pool. Count your strokes. Try for an average of 6 feet or more per stroke.

Success Goal = 6 feet per stroke ___

Success Check
- Wide step, bottom leg way back on kick ___
- Powerful top-hand push ___
- Streamlined glide ___

To Increase Difficulty
- Try for glides averaging 8 feet.
- Control your side-float position by bending or arching as needed to maintain balance.

To Decrease Difficulty
- Wear a float belt.
- Decrease the goal glide length.

With a skilled swimmer watching you, start at the deep end of the pool. Push off and swim to the shallow end. Count your strokes. Try to average 6 feet or more per stroke.

Success Goal = 25 yards in 12 strokes ___

Success Check
• Use a smooth, fully coordinate stroke ___
• Keep your ear in the water and streamline your body and legs for the glide ___

To Increase Difficulty
• Try to do 25 yards in 10 strokes.

To Decrease Difficulty
• Stay close to the pool edge.
• Wear a float belt.
• Have a skilled swimmer hold a float belt and swim with you.

Swim the sidestroke across the pool using only your legs and forward arm. With your top arm, hold a 10-pound diving brick or similar weight item on top of your hip. Do not try to glide, but alternate stroking and kicking continuously.

Success Goal = 1 pool width or 15 yards carrying 10 pounds ___

Success Check
• Use a quick, powerful pull of your forward arm ___
• Alternate kick and pull with no glide ___

To Increase Difficulty
• Carry 15 pounds.
• See how much you can carry.

To Decrease Difficulty
• Carry only 5 pounds.
• Tow a large floating object instead.

SIDESTROKE SUCCESS SUMMARY

You now know the power of the side stroke, but it doesn't have to be a power stroke all the time. You can also use it as an easy stroke to eat up great distances. Let your head float comfortably on the water with your mouth clear to breathe and take long restful glides to swim over long distances. Before you move to the next step, however, have a knowledgeable friend or instructor evaluate your technique. Compare your methods with the techniques described in Figures 8.1, 8.2, and 8.3.

Now you know a power stroke, but how about swimming for speed? Turn the page and begin to learn the king of speed strokes—the crawl.

STEP 9

CRAWL STROKE:

REAL SWIMMING

AKE YOUR MARK!—Eight swimmers step to the front of the starting block, and an electronic beep sends them coursing down the pool in the 100-meter freestyle race. Matt Biondi returns in only 48.42 seconds to become the world's fastest freestyle swimmer. Jenny Thompson swam the same distance in 54.48 seconds to become the women's 100-meter freestyle world record holder. With some practice, *you* can swim with the freestyle champions! Freestyle? What kind of swimming stroke is that?

The rule book says that a freestyle race may be swum in any style or stroke the swimmer desires. Without exception, the choice of stroke for the freestyle race is the crawl stroke. The words *freestyle* and *crawl stroke* are practically synonymous.

The crawl stroke. Now that's *real* swimming—the fastest swimming stroke known.

Overhand Arm Stroke

The crawl stroke employs an overhand arm stroke in which the arm recovers over the water instead of pushing through it. Because you have learned the side-glide position, the overhand arm stroke will be an easy transition for you. Please remember, though, that you can't have an arm *and* your mouth out of water at the same time without additional support. The overhand arm stroke requires precise timing to allow you to breathe during the pull of the breathing-side arm.

Why Is the Overhand Stroke Important?

The overhand stroke is important to you because it will allow you, for the first time, to employ the pull with no underwater resistance on the recovery. You will not save much energy, because it will require as much energy to lift the arm as to push it through the water, but you will gain a great deal of efficiency for the same effort.

How to Do the Overhand (Crawl) Arm Stroke

Attach a deep-float leg float to one ankle. Push off the wall in a face-down position. Pull through with the breathing-side arm into a side-glide position. Allow the trailing hand to rest on your thigh, but turn it *palm up*. Recover by lifting your elbow. Allow your hand to be fully relaxed, fingers trailing at the surface. Your elbow should bend about 90 degrees and lead the hand until your arm is at shoulder height (see Figure 9.1a). Stay in the side-glide position and keep your elbow higher than your hand as your hand passes your face (see Figure 9.1b). Reach forward with your hand, but keep your shoulder and elbow up. Place your hand in the water as far in front as you can reach, but move as if you were reaching over a barrel lying on its side in front of your head (see Figure 9.1c). Fingertips should touch the water before your elbow. Roll your face down and glide on the recovering arm as you begin your pull with the opposite arm (see Figure 9.1d). Repeat the roll and arm action on the other side, except that your face will stay under the water. Don't allow the position of your face to keep you from rolling fully to the side in that direction. Stay on your side until your hand passes your head with the elbow high enough to reach over the barrel on that side.

FIGURE
9.1

FIGURE
9.1 **KEYS TO SUCCESS**

OVERHAND ARM STROKE
Execution

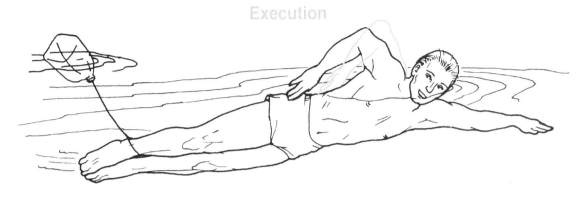

a

1. Inhale. Turn the palm up on your trailing arm ___
2. Lift your elbow; allow your hand to trail ___

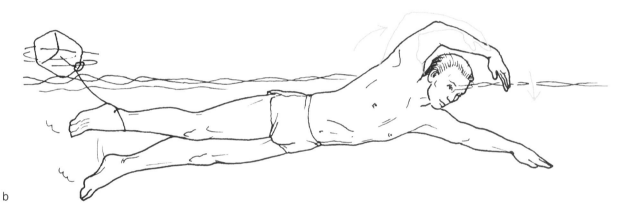

b

3. Your elbow should be bent 90 degrees as your hand passes your face ___

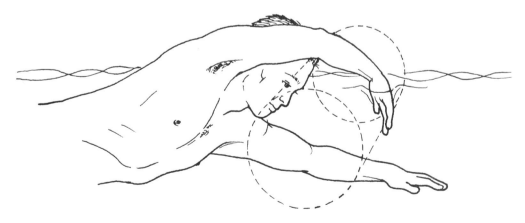

c

4. Reach forward over the barrel ___

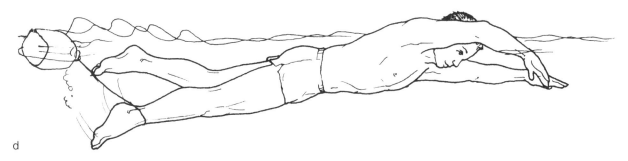

d

5. Your fingers should touch the water before your elbow ___
6. Roll face down, stretch, glide, both arms in front ___
7. Pull through to a side glide on the other side, keep your face down and exhale ___
8. Recover the other arm in the same manner ___

Crawl Stroke

Now we must package an arm stroke, a leg kick, and a breathing pattern into the crawl stroke. A few modifications will be necessary to the techniques you have been using.

Why Is the Crawl Stroke Important?

The crawl stroke is the very essence of the image of swimming. It will move you through the water faster than any other stroke, while allowing you to see where you are going. The crawl will not *save* energy, and for survival you will turn to other strokes, but it *uses* energy most efficiently. Nevertheless, it will be your stroke of choice anytime you decide to go swimming. Two modifications are necessary to combine the skills you have learned into the crawl-stroke package. You must start to pull one arm just as the opposite hand enters the water, and you must coordinate your kick with your armstroke so that you kick three times with each arm pull.

How to Swim the Crawl Stroke

Starting from the prone-float position, begin kicking and counting each downward thrust of each foot. Count in sets of six kicks. Emphasize counts one and four thus: ONE-two-three, FOUR-five-six. After two complete sets of kicks, begin the pull of the non-breathing-side arm on the count of one (see Figure 9.2a). Pull completely through, exhale, and recover on the counts of two and three (see Figure 9.2b). As you count three, the recovering hand should be passing your head on the way to entering the water, elbow high (see Figure 9.2c). On the count of four, the recovering hand drops into the water, fingertips first, and the breathing-side arm begins its pull simultaneously (see Figure 9.2d). On the count of five the breathing-side arm pulls through, and you inhale (see Figure 9.2e). On the count of six the arm recovers to the level of your head, ready to enter the water, elbow high. On the count of one, your breathing-side hand enters the water, fingertips first, and you begin the pull with the opposite arm simultaneously (see Figure 9.2f).

Recapping, the hands enter the water on counts ONE and FOUR. Exhale on counts two and three; inhale on counts five and six. The feet kick steadily without hesitation or change in rhythm.

FIGURE 9.2

KEYS TO SUCCESS

CRAWL STROKE—NON-BREATHING SIDE

Execution

(On kick number . . .)

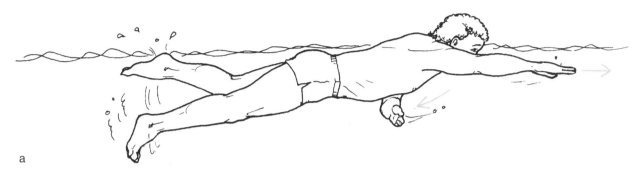

a

1. ONE—pull with your non-breathing arm; exhale ___

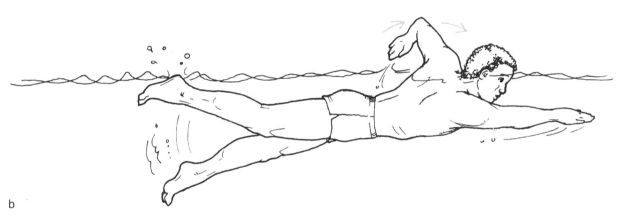

b

2. Two—recover your non-breathing arm; elbow high ___

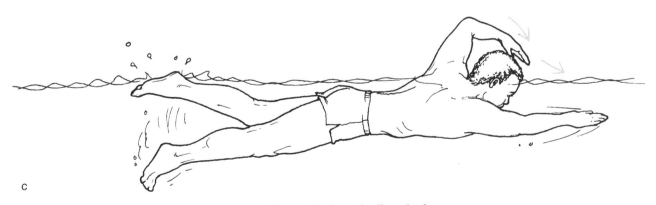

c

3. Three—reach over the barrel; elbow high ___

CRAWL STROKE—BREATHING SIDE

Execution

(On kick number . . .)

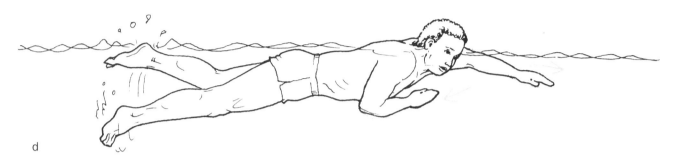

d

1. FOUR—non-breathing hand enters water; start pulling with your breathing arm ___

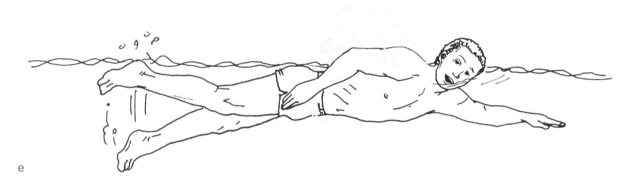

e

2. Five—inhale on the last half of the pull of your breathing arm; elbow high ___

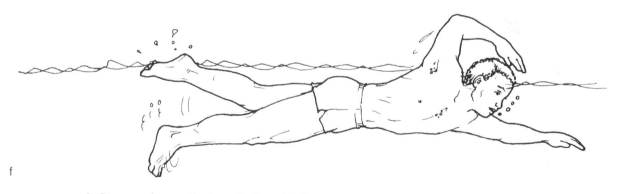

f

3. Six—reach over the barrel; elbow high ___
4. ONE—hand enters the water; start the pull of your non-breathing arm ___
5. Continue rhythmically ___

CRAWL STROKE SUCCESS STOPPERS

Coordinating the overhand stroke with your kicking and breathing is a little complicated. Errors creep into the coordination process. Here are some corrections for the common errors.

ERROR	CORRECTION
Overhand Stroke	
1. You are getting water when you try to breathe.	1. Breathe during the last half of the pull.
2. Your elbow touches before your fingertips.	2. Stay in the side-glide position longer; keep your shoulder high.
3. Your elbow drops and your hand leads on the recovery.	3. Relax your wrist; trail your fingertips along the surface of the water.
4. Your hand is palm down on the recovery.	4. Finish the pull with your palm up.
5. Your hand enters the water at your head.	5. Reach forward, over the barrel.
6. Your lower arm is pulling during the recovery of the upper arm.	6. Glide on your lower arm.
7. Your feet sink.	7. Pull back on the water, not down; keep your ear under water.
Crawl Stroke	
1. You are pulling too wide.	1. Keep your hand under the centerline of your body.
2. You are dropping your elbow too soon.	2. Hold the shoulder-high side position longer.
3. Your palm faces down at the beginning of your recovery.	3. Relax your wrist; let your fingers trail.
4. Coordination between your arms and your feet is wrong.	4. Slow down; start over; count.

CRAWL STROKE

DRILLS

1. Overhand Drill, Breathing Side, With Support

Use the deep-float leg support on your breathing-side ankle. Hold a kickboard in your opposite hand—fingers on top of the board and thumb underneath. Assume a side-glide position, ear on extended forward arm. Go through the motions of the overhand recovery in slow motion and watch the recovering arm (review Figure 9.1). Roll onto your stomach as your hand enters the water. Stretch your breathing arm forward as you exhale. Pull with the same arm again. Inhale during the last half of the pull. Stop and float in the side-glide position. Repeat using only your breathing arm. Repeat. Repeat.

Success Goal = 10 consecutive breathing-arm strokes ___

Success Check

- Inhale on the pull as you roll to a side glide ___
- Lift your elbow, hand trailing, palm up ___
- Keep your elbow high and leading your hand until your elbow reaches shoulder level ___
- Reach forward over the barrel, elbow high, wrist relaxed; elbow higher than fingertips ___
- *Then* roll face down as your hand enters the water and stretches forward to glide ___

To Increase Difficulty

- Eliminate leg support.
- Increase the goal to 15 consecutive strokes.

To Decrease Difficulty

- Pause momentarily in side-glide position with hand on thigh and palm up.
- Use a pull-buoy-type leg float.

2. Overhand Stroke, Non-Breathing Side, With Support

Repeat Drill 1 on the opposite side. Keep your face out of water during the recovery so you can see the arm motion. Attach the float to the other ankle (upper leg), keep lower ear under water, and exhale as your hand enters the water and stretches. Inhale on the last half of the pull. Use only the non-breathing-side arm, but breathe on each pull, again and again.

Success Goal = 10 consecutive non-breathing-arm strokes ___

Success Check

- Check items are the same as for the previous drill ___

To Increase Difficulty

- Eliminate the leg float.
- Eliminate the kickboard.

To Decrease Difficulty

- Use a pull-buoy-type leg float.
- Wear a float belt.

3. Overhand Stroke, Both Arms, With Support

Start as above, using the leg float on one ankle. As the recovering arm reaches forward, take hold of the kickboard with that hand and release it from the other hand. Now pull with the opposite arm and recover. Keep changing hands with the kickboard as each arm reaches forward. Breathe *only* on the regular breathing side; keep your face in the water during the recovery of the opposite arm. Exhale during the pull of the non-breathing-side arm. Try to move in slow motion. Keep your feet fairly close. Do not "swim," just *float* along and pull with both arms alternately.

Success Goal = 10 consecutive arm strokes ___

Success Check
- Arms pull exactly as in the basic arm pull; only the recovery and body roll change ___
- Feet remain still ___
- Good rhythm without hesitation ___

To Increase Difficulty
- Eliminate the kickboard.
- Eliminate the leg float.
- Do 10 armstrokes with each arm.

To Decrease Difficulty
- Wear goggles if you wish.
- Use a pull-buoy-type leg float.

4. Touch and Go Overhand Stroke With Leg Support

Repeat Drill 3, but without the kickboard. Use the leg-support float again. Start pulling with the arm opposite the breathing arm. Exhale during the pull. Be sure to keep the forward arm straight and stretched until the recovering hand stretches forward and touches it. Thus "touch" the forward hand to tell it when to "go." Continue touch-and-go alternate overhand stroking. Breathe only on the regular breathing side, but breathe *every time* that arm pulls. Breathe on the pull, *not* on the recovery.

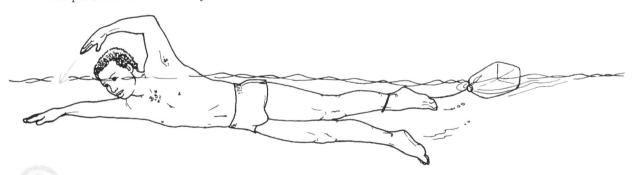

Success Goal = 10 consecutive touch-and-go strokes, 5 with each arm ___

Success Check
- Begin to roll as you begin to pull on each side ___
- Exhale on the non-breathing-arm pull ___
- Inhale on the breathing-arm pull ___
- Pull under your centerline, elbow bent 90 degrees ___

To Increase Difficulty
- Continue for 20 strokes, 10 with each arm.
- Breathe on the opposite side.

To Decrease Difficulty
- Wear goggles.
- Stop momentarily at the touch of each hand.
- Wear a float belt.

Repeat Drill 4 without the leg support. Allow your legs to kick for support.

Success Goal = 10 touch-and-go strokes ___

Success Check
* Breathe only on the pull of the breathing arm ___
* Each hand touches the other before it begins to pull ___
* Begin to roll as each arm begins to pull ___
* Pull in the center line of your body ___

To Increase Difficulty
* Breathe on the opposite side.
* Do 20 touch-and-go strokes.
* Kick six kicks per two arm strokes, touch on kick counts one and four.

To Decrease Difficulty
* Wear goggles.
* Start kicking before you start to pull.
* Pull back; don't press down.

With a skilled swimmer or lifeguard watching you, start at the deep end of the pool and swim an overhand stroke to the shallow end. Continue to touch and go. Kick to support your feet.

Success Goal = 1 pool length or 25 yards ___

Success Check
* Use long, full arm pulls ___
* Pull in the center line of your body ___
* Breathe during the pull of your breathing arm ___
* Touch each hand before it pulls ___

To Increase Difficulty
* Turn and swim back again for 50 yards.
* Count six kicks for each complete (two arms) stroke.

To Decrease Difficulty
* Wear a float belt.
* Wear goggles.
* Stay close to an edge, or swim with a guard.

Don a mask and snorkel. With a skilled swimmer or lifeguard watching you, use the overhand stroke to swim the length of the pool. Start at the deep end. Remember to keep your face in the water, but inhale on the pull of your breathing arm and exhale on the pull of the opposite arm. Turn your body nearly into side-float position for the arm recovery on each side.

Success Goal = 1 pool length with 100% *good* overhand recoveries ___

Success Check
- Breathe only through your mouth, but keep your breathing rhythm ___
- Keep your face down so the snorkel remains clear ___
- Roll your body *nearly* into side-float position ___
- Maintain the touch-and-go arm stroke ___

To Increase Difficulty
- Count six kick beats; hands touch on one and four.
- Turn and swim back again.

To Decrease Difficulty
- Stay close to the edge.
- Swim with a skilled swimmer.

8. Crawl Stroke Kick

Modify the kick you have been using. Hold a kickboard with both hands extended in front of you. Start with a prone glide and kick easily. Make your kick very narrow. Keep your knees fairly straight; kick your whole leg from the hip with loose, floppy ankles. Only your heels should break the surface. Tilt your head to the front to inhale and drop your face into the water to exhale. Count each downward kick. *Begin your count with the leg on the breathing side* and count in sets of six, with emphasis on the counts of ONE and FOUR. Kick for propulsion, but if your ankles are stiff and do not point well, you will get very little forward movement. You should, however, be able to get enough support to keep your feet near the surface. Pressing too hard on the kickboard will make your feet sink.

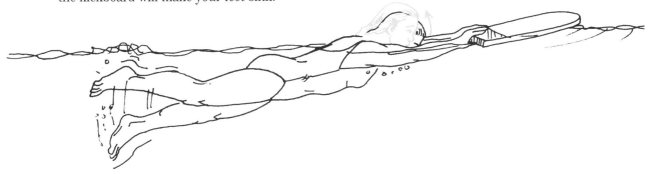

Success Goal = 1 pool width or 15 yards ___

Success Check
- Use a small kick, knees almost straight ___
- Let your ankles relax; let your feet flop ___
- Kick from the hip, not the knee ___
- Count your kicks in sets of six ___
- Emphasize kick beats ONE and FOUR ___
- Begin the count with a breathing-side leg kick ___

To Increase Difficulty
- Increase the distance to 30 yards.

To Decrease Difficulty
- Wear a mask and snorkel and keep your face down.
- Lift *up* on the kickboard to keep your feet up.

9. Crawl Stroke Kick With Fins and Kickboard

Don a pair of swim fins. Wear a pair of athletic socks in the swim fins to prevent chafing by fins that may not fit exactly. Repeat Drill 8 with fins. Hold a kickboard with both hands extended in front of you. Do not try to kick the fins. Kick your legs from the hips with straight knees and let the fins do whatever they wish. Your ankles *must* be relaxed so the fins can flop properly to furnish propulsion. You will be aware of a tremendous increase in propulsion. Count your kicks in groups of six, with emphasis on counts ONE and FOUR, *beginning with the breathing-side leg.*

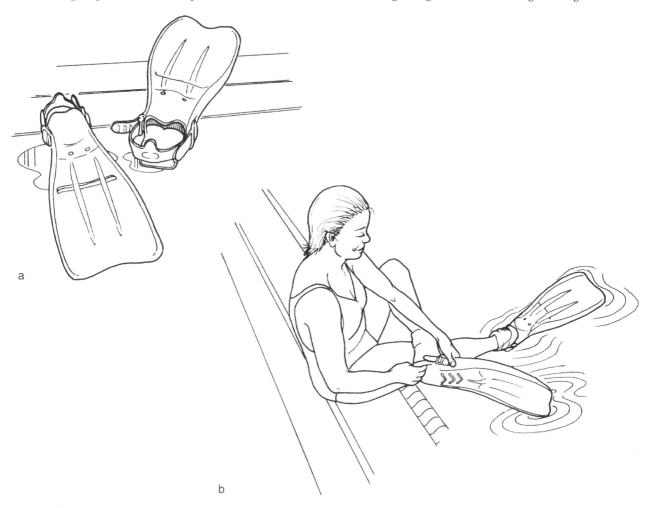

a

b

Success Goal = 1 pool width or 15 yards ___

Success Check
• Kick your legs, not the fins ___
• Your ankles are relaxed and floppy ___
• Tilt your head; thrust your chin forward to breathe ___
• Count your kicks in sets of six ___
• Begin the count with your breathing-side leg ___
• Emphasize kick beats ONE and FOUR ___

To Increase Difficulty
• Discard the kickboard; scull with your hands to raise your head for breathing.
• Increase the distance to 30 yards.

To Decrease Difficulty
• Wear a mask and snorkel; keep your face down.
• Kick slowly; resist the urge to go fast.

10. Crawl Stroke Kick With Fins, Breathing-Side Pull

Wearing fins, but without the kickboard, begin to kick as in Drill 9. Exhale underwater on the first set of six kicks. On the second set of six kicks, begin to pull on the count of FOUR with the breathing arm only. Use the overhand stroke recovery. Roll and breathe as you pull on counts FOUR and five (see Figure a). Recover over the water on count six, and return the arm to the water on count ONE (see Figure b). Exhale as you glide on counts ONE, two, and three with arms stretched overhead. Pull and breathe again on the breathing side on counts FOUR and five. Recover over the water on six and return your arm to the water on count ONE. Continue. Pull only on the breathing side. Roll fully into the side-glide position to facilitate breathing, but do not pause in the side-glide position. Continue the rhythm of the kick.

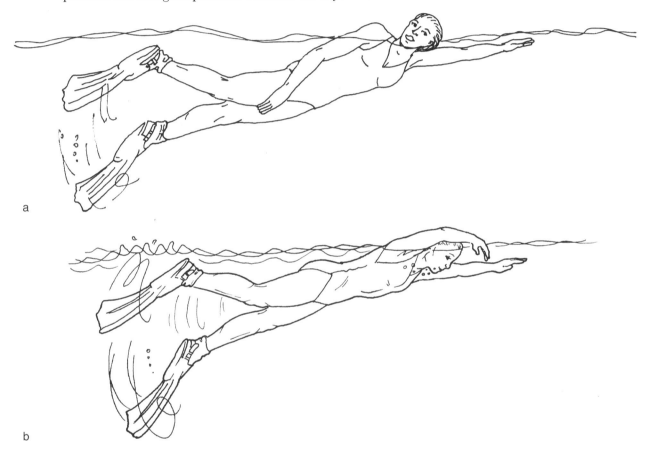

a

b

Success Goal = 15 yards ___

Success Check
- Kick in steady rhythm ___
- Inhale on count five while still pulling ___
- Exhale on counts ONE, two, three ___
- Pull with the breathing arm again and again ___

To Increase Difficulty
- Extend the goal distance to 30 yards.
- Repeat drill without fins.

To Decrease Difficulty
- Hold a kickboard in your nonbreathing hand during the drill.
- Wear a mask and snorkel. Keep your face down, but inhale and exhale exactly on the correct counts.

11. Coordinated Crawl Stroke

Begin with a prone glide, kicking your legs. Begin kicking and counting with the foot on the breathing side. Stretch your arms in front and hold your breath through a full sequence of six kicks. Begin to exhale and pull with the nonbreathing arm on the second count of ONE. Pull through and start recovery on counts two and three. As your arm returns to the water on count FOUR, begin the pull of the breathing-side arm. Inhale on count five. Bring that arm over the water on count six; reach forward into the water as you begin the pull of the nonbreathing arm on ONE. Be sure to return that arm to the water exactly on the count of ONE, as you begin the second pull of the nonbreathing arm. Slow to slow motion; float along and concentrate on the coordination between arms and legs.

Success Goal = 10 completely coordinated strokes ___

Success Check
• Float and kick in slow motion ___
• Begin counting ONE with the kick of the breathing-side leg, as the nonbreathing arm starts pulling; exhale ___
• Pull and recover the nonbreathing arm on counts two and three; arm enters the water on FOUR ___
• Pull with the breathing arm on FOUR, inhale on five, bring the arm over on six; arm enters the water on ONE ___

To Increase Difficulty
• Continue very slowly for 20 strokes.
• Slowly begin to increase your speed; maintain correct coordination.

To Decrease Difficulty
• Wear a mask and snorkel and keep your face down, but breathe in proper coordination.
• Move very, very slowly; just float.
• Roll your body, but keep your face in the water.

Begin swimming a completely coordinated crawl stroke. On the second or third stroke, inhale on the count of five and pause in a side-glide position on the count of six. Your hand should be resting on your thigh, and you are not kicking. Resume after a pause of 2 seconds; pause again on the count of three in a side-glide position on the opposite side. Your hand should be resting on your thigh, and you are face down. Resume again after 2 seconds. Continue to swim a hesitation stroke, stopping all motion for 2 seconds on counts six and three.

Success Goal = 10 consecutive hesitation arm strokes in side-glide position ___

Success Check
• Inhale deeply on count five and hold your breath during the hesitation ___
• Exhale on counts two and three and during that hesitation ___
• Roll onto your side while pulling with each arm ___

To Increase Difficulty
• Breathe on both sides.
• Increase the number of strokes to 20.

To Decrease Difficulty
• Wear a mask and snorkel and keep your face down, but roll and breathe in correct coordination.
• Wear a float belt.
• Wear swim fins.

13. Deep-Water Crawl Stroke

With a lifeguard watching, crawl stroke from the shallow end of the pool to the deep end, make a wide turn, and swim back to the shallow end.

Success Goal = 2 pool lengths or 50 yards, with a wide turn ____

Success Check
- Use long, full strokes ____
- Inhale on every breathing-arm pull ____
- Reach to the side and pull in that direction to turn ____

To Increase Difficulty
- On the second length breathe on the opposite side.
- Breathe every *third* stroke (on alternate sides).

To Decrease Difficulty
- Wear goggles.
- Wear swim fins.

14. Crawl Stroke for Distance With Open Turn

With a lifeguard watching you, begin swimming the crawl stroke at the shallow end of the pool. Swim to the deep end, turn on your side, grasp the edge with your leading hand, tuck your feet, and pivot *vertically* (bringing your feet down under you). Place your feet against the wall, put both hands in front of you, face down, and push off. Glide for 2 seconds before resuming the crawl stroke. Swim back to the shallow end, repeat the turn, push off, and continue swimming lengths.

Success Goal = 4 pool lengths or 100 yards ____

Success Check
- Use long, full strokes ____
- Pivot *vertically* on the turn ____
- Glide on each arm until the opposite hand touches the water ____

To Increase Difficulty
- Change your breathing side from time to time.
- Have someone time you for 100 yards.
- Add swim fins and have someone time you.

To Decrease Difficulty
- Wear goggles and/or swim fins.
- Swim slowly; stroke in time to your breathing needs, not vice versa.

CRAWL STROKE SUCCESS SUMMARY

If you want to swim in competition, now is the time to enter training for freestyle competition. Have a swimming coach evaluate your crawl stroke and make suggestions for your training. Join a competitive swim club and begin regular workouts. Your improvement will be rapid.

If you are not inclined toward competition, have a knowledgeable friend use the keys to success in Figures 9.1 and 9.2 to evaluate your crawl stroke. Continue to practice under guidance to perfect your stroke.

STEP
10
ELEMENTARY BACKSTROKE: A NEW KICK

S hifting from the swift-moving crawl stroke to the easy, lazy elementary backstroke requires a startling change of pace. We will leave the pursuit of competitive swimming temporarily to add a new kick-and-survival stroke to your swimming repertoire. The breaststroke kick as used in the elementary backstroke will be important to you when we return to competitive swimming strokes in the next step.

The elementary backstroke is similar to the basic backstroke you have been swimming; in fact, the arm stroke is identical. The leg kick and timing are quite different, however. In addition, this stroke introduces an entirely new foot and leg motion.

Why Is the Elementary Backstroke Important?

The elementary backstroke is one of the recognized package strokes because of its ease and efficiency. It is efficient not for its *use* of energy, but for its *conservation* of energy. Its greater importance, however, lies in the fact that the elementary backstroke is the most efficient way to introduce the breaststroke kick.

We have been minimizing the importance of the kick in some of the strokes introduced to this point, but in strokes that use the breaststroke kick (elementary backstroke and breaststroke) the kick produces as much propulsion as the arms.

The breaststroke kick is a completely unique motion. You should be cautioned against vigorous practice of the kick until your muscles have time to adjust. Its efficiency depends upon the flexibility in your knee and ankle.

How to Swim the Elementary Backstroke

From a back-float position begin the recovery of your arms. As the arms recover, drop your heels down with your ankles fully hooked. Do not sit or bend at the hips (see Figure 10.1a). As your hands turn outward for the arm extension, turn your still-hooked feet outward as far as possible. Your knees will separate somewhat to achieve this position, but should remain fairly close together. As your arms stretch outward, move your feet out wider than the knees, toes first. As you begin to pull, your feet continue to move outward. The knees now separate, still bent to maximum flexion; toes point out, and ankles are fully hooked (see Figure 10.1b). In midpull, push backward and squeeze in a circular motion with the inside of your hooked foot and ankle. Your ankle extends, and your toes point at the very end of the kick. The kick and arm stroke finish at about the same time, but the arms may finish just slightly after the kick. Remain streamlined, but relaxed, for a long glide (see Figure 10.1c).

FIGURE
10.1

KEYS TO SUCCESS

ELEMENTARY BACKSTROKE
Execution

| ***Arms do this*** | ***while*** | ***Feet do this*** |

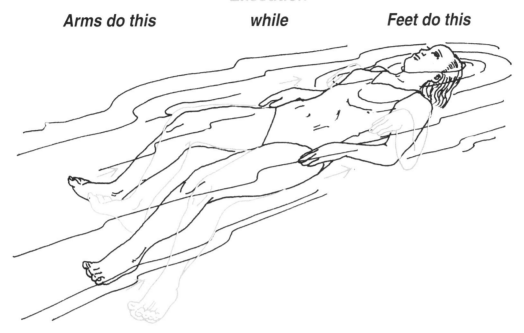

a

1. Arms recover; thumbs along side ___
2. Hands at shoulders; fingers point out ___

1. Heels drop; ankles hook ___
2. Ankles hooked; toes pointed out ___

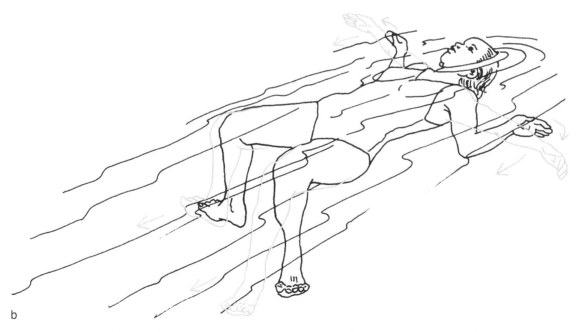

b

3. Arms extend for catch ___
4. Arms begin pull ___

3. Feet move out, toes first ___
4. Feet move out and around ___

Arms do this   **while**   **Feet do this**

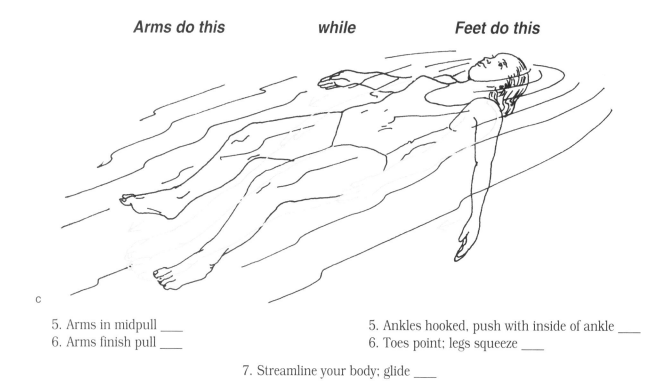

c

5. Arms in midpull ___	5. Ankles hooked, push with inside of ankle ___
6. Arms finish pull ___	6. Toes point; legs squeeze ___

7. Streamline your body; glide ___

ELEMENTARY BACKSTROKE SUCCESS STOPPERS

Learning to recognize a well-executed elementary backstroke is easier if you can compare correct and incorrect movements. We list the most common errors with corresponding suggestions on how to correct them.

ERROR	CORRECTION
1. Your knees break the surface.	1. Arch; do not bend at the hips; drop your heels behind you.
2. Water washes over your face on the recovery.	2. Recover slowly, *sneak* your hands up your sides, keep knees under water, lift your chin.
3. Water washes over your face on the pull.	3. Tilt your chin down slightly; pull level, not upward.
4. You get no power from your kick.	4. *Hook* your ankles; push with the inside of your foot; kick wide and squeeze.
5. Your arms and legs do not finish at the same time.	5. Start pulling slightly ahead of your kick.
6. You stroke rapidly.	6. Ride your glide until your body motion slows.
7. Your legs begin to sink.	7. You are riding your glide too long; stroke sooner.

DRILLS

1. Elementary Backstroke Kick, Land Drill

Sit at the edge of the pool deck with your legs over the water to midthigh. Lean back on your arms. Hook your ankles as far as you can; hold that position as you drop your heels behind you. (A low pool deck will allow your feet to be in the water.) Put your heels against the wall and turn your toes outward as far as you can. Keep your knees fairly close but allow them to separate as far as they must to get the toes pointed outward. Move each foot in a half-circle simultaneously: out, around, push back, and together—squeezing at the very last part of the movement. Keep your ankles hooked and feel the push of the water on the inside of your feet. Point your toes and streamline your legs as your feet touch.

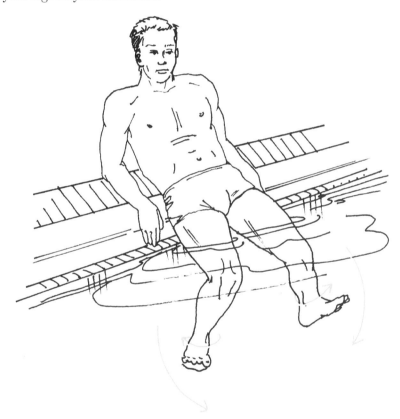

Success Goal = 10 powerful backward thrusts with the inside of your feet ____

Success Check
- Hook your ankles; keep your knees fairly close ____
- Drop your heels down behind you ____
- Turn your toes out; kick out, around, and push the water back with the inside of your feet ____
- Squeeze your feet together; toes point; stretch ____

To Increase Difficulty
- Keep your knees close together as your feet separate with ankles hooked.
- Drive water directly backward with your feet.

To Decrease Difficulty
- Move very slowly with no thrust on first trials.
- Allow your knees to separate widely to gain proper foot position.

2. Elementary Backstroke Kick Drill, Bracketed on the Pool Edge, Arms Wide

In shallow water place your back against the pool wall. Reach back and outward to place your arms and elbows on the edge of the pool. Bend 90 degrees at the waist and hold your feet out in front of you. With knees about 4 inches apart, stay bent at the hips, but bend your knees and drop both heels toward the bottom of the pool. Hook your ankles as your feet drop. Keep your ankles hooked and turn your toes outward as far as they will go. Catch the water with the inside of your foot; push it in a circle: out, around, back, and together as your knees straighten. Point your toes at the very last moment and try to put the bottoms of your feet together. Try to prolong the kick with your toes and the bottom of your feet. It is important for your feet to move outward *before* your knees at the beginning of the kick.

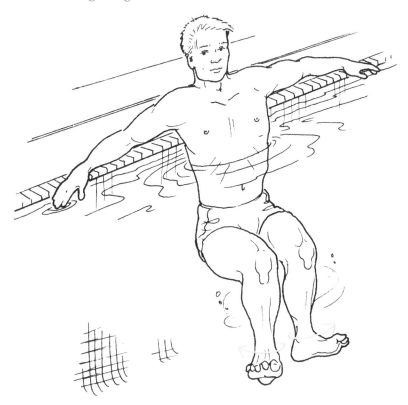

Success Goal = 10 kicks that tend to push you tighter against the wall ___

Success Check
• Keep your back against the wall and your legs straight out in front; hook your ankles ___
• Drop your heels straight down behind you ___
• Keep your knees close, turn your toes outward ___
• Move your feet outward, leading the knees apart ___
• Thrust directly back with the inside of your feet ___
• Squeeze: knees straight, toes pointed ___

To Increase Difficulty
• Keep your knees about 4 inches apart while your hooked ankles move out and around.
• Increase your success goal to 20 kicks.

To Decrease Difficulty
• If your pool has a high edge, use the overflow trough or a ladder at water level.
• Move in slow motion, examine each leg position.

3. Elementary Backstroke Kick Drill Against Pressure

Repeat Drill 2. Ask a friend to stand in front of you and place one hand against the inside of each of your feet, fingers under the arch. Push around and back against the hands. *CAUTION—PRESS VERY LIGHTLY, THESE ARE WEAK MUSCLES!*

Success Goal = 10 kicks that give you the feeling of backward pressure ___

Success Check
- Push lightly back against your friend's hands ___
- Experience the feeling of pressure against the inside of your ankles ___

To Increase Difficulty
- Ask your friend to increase the resistance gradually.
- After 10 kicks, ask your friend to step aside while you make 5 additional kicks. Recover slowly and push quickly and forcefully each time.

To Decrease Difficulty
- Have your friend move backward as you press.
- Push lightly to avoid muscle strain.
- Reduce the goal to 6 kicks.

Hold a kickboard fairly close to your chest in shallow water. Float on your back—hips elevated and straight. Keep your knees about 4 inches apart; drop your heels back under you as far as you can with the ankle fully hooked. Turn your toes outward. Make sure the feet lead the knees as you kick out, around, back, and together with the side of your foot. Kick very wide, legs separating widely, and squeeze together as you straighten your knees and point your toes at the end of the kick. Glide to a full stop.

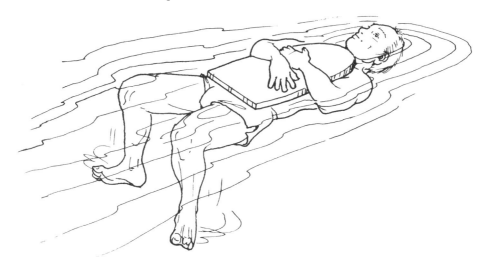

Success Goal = 15 yards of head-first progress ___

Success Check
• Keep your hips straight; do not sit ___
• Flex ankles fully; drop heels; turn toes out ___
• Kick out wide and back to full extension ___
• Point your toes and stretch for a glide ___

To Increase Difficulty
• Use a slow recovery and a whip kick; try to average a distance of 2 yards per kick.
• Speed up the recovery to make the kick a smooth, continuous motion. Glide.

To Decrease Difficulty
• Start in slow motion and build to a quick kick.
• Recover slowly, then whip your feet out and around.

5. Coordinated Elementary Backstroke

Without the kickboard, float on your back, arms outstretched and slightly above shoulder level. Hook your ankles, drop your heels, and turn your toes outward. Begin a full arm pull; then deliver the kick. Try to finish the pull and kick simultaneously. Glide until your forward motion slows. Recover your arms by sliding your hands up along your sides. Simultaneously begin to drop your heels behind you. As your hands turn out and start to reach up and out; turn your toes outward. Then pull and kick (review Figure 10.1).

Success Goal = 10 full pulls and kicks with glide ___

Success Check
- Start to pull just before starting the kick ___
- Finish the kick and pull together ___
- Glide, long and streamlined ___
- Recover your arms and legs together ___

To Increase Difficulty
- Ride your glide to a complete stop.
- Scull while gliding.

To Decrease Difficulty
- Recover slowly, kick and pull vigorously.
- Inhale on the recovery; exhale on the pull.

6. Elementary Backstroke, Distance per Stroke

Repeat Drill 5 with emphasis on distance traveled per stroke. Ride each glide for maximum distance: remain streamlined, but relaxed. Stretch for greater arm reach on the pull. Pull and kick with strength; then relax for rest.

Success Goal = 10 feet per stroke across the pool ___

Success Check
- Pull with level, smooth pull ___
- Glide with hands at your sides and toes pointed ___

To Increase Difficulty
- Reach higher for a longer pull.
- Recover your legs more quickly, just before the pull.

To Decrease Difficulty
- Keep your chin down on the pull, up for the glide.
- Make sure your pull is level.

7. Elementary Backstroke With Turn

In shallow water push off the side wall in back-glide position. Begin a coordinated elementary backstroke. Near the opposite side, stop kicking. Stroke with one arm only and make a wide turn. Swim back to the start.

Success Goal = 2 pool widths or 30 yards with a smooth turn ___

Success Check

• Push off with hands at your sides ___
• Turn with one arm at your side ___
• Do not kick while turning, keep legs streamlined ___

To Increase Difficulty

• Make a full 360-degree turn in the middle of the pool.
• Make a second turn in the opposite direction and increase the distance to 45 yards.

To Decrease Difficulty

• Hold a deep breath during most of the turn.
• Do not glide after arm strokes while turning.

8. Elementary Backstroke for Distance

With a lifeguard watching you, start swimming at the shallow end of the pool. Push off the wall in a back-glide position and swim a fully coordinated elementary backstroke to the deep end or about 25 yards. Make a wide turn and swim back to the starting point. Turn again and continue for a total of four pool lengths or about 100 yards (with three turns).

Success Goal = 100 yards and three turns ___

Success Check

• Take long, full pulls ___
• End your kick and arm stroke simultaneously ___
• Relax on your long glides ___
• Don't kick during the turns ___
• Pull one arm with no glide on turns ___

To Increase Difficulty

• Alternate the direction of your turns.
• Increase the goal to 200 yards.

To Decrease Difficulty

• Swim slowly with long glides.
• Wear a float belt for security.

9. Combine Crawl Stroke and Elementary Backstroke

With a lifeguard watching you, swim the crawl stroke from the shallow end to the deep end of the pool. Make a wide turn and turn over onto your back. Swim elementary backstroke back to the shallow end. Make a wide turn while on your back, then turn over, and swim crawl stroke to the deep end again. Grasp the end of the pool, turn, push off on your back, and use the elementary backstroke to return to the shallow end.

Success Goal = 100 yards nonstop swimming with 3 turns; alternate between crawl stroke and elementary backstroke ____

Success Check
- Make the first turn while swimming crawl stroke, the second turn while swimming elementary backstroke, and the third turn by grasping the wall ____
- Swim smoothly; breathe rhythmically ____
- Use long, full pulls and long glides ____

To Increase Difficulty
- Make your first turn to the right and the second turn to the left.
- Alternate breathing sides during the crawl stroke.

To Decrease Difficulty
- Wear goggles.
- Wear a float belt for security.
- Swim beside a skilled swimmer.
- After each turn onto your back, float and rest for a short period.

ELEMENTARY BACKSTROKE SUCCESS SUMMARY

The kick you have learned for the elementary backstroke is identical to the breaststroke kick. Learn it well before continuing. Have a knowledgeable swimmer or instructor critique your elementary backstroke using the keys to success criteria in Figure 10.1. This stroke is invaluable for conserving energy in a critical situation.

BREASTSTROKE:

HEADS UP

The breaststroke is an ancient swimming stroke with roots traceable to biblical times. It has survived through the ages and is recognized today as one of the four strokes used in international swimming competition. World records in the 200-meter breaststroke are currently held by U.S. swimmers Mike Barrowman (2 minutes, 10.16 seconds—men) and Anita Nall (2 minutes, 25.35 seconds—women). The breaststroke is subject to more restrictions and qualifying rules than any other stroke and is defined very precisely in the rule books.

Despite its precise definition, the breaststroke is easy and comfortable to swim. When properly swum, it requires rhythmic breathing with the face submerged during the glide. However, it adapts very easily to a semivertical position with the head held up to allow the swimmer to see and to converse with others. It is, therefore, often called the "social" or the "conversational" stroke.

The breaststroke pull is a rather short and somewhat ineffective pull that seems contrary to the principle that "long, full arm motions are best." It is necessary to keep this pull short and sharp, however, because of the way it coordinates with the kick.

As the propulsive arm motion of a competitive swimming stroke, the breaststroke arm pull is important, but the breaststroke is a very kick-intensive stroke in which the kick provides as much or more propulsion than the arm pull. The importance of the arm pull, then, is not so much for the propulsion it pro-

vides, as for the role it plays as the basis and support of the kick that follows.

How to Execute the Breaststroke Pull

Start from a prone float with arms extended. Flex your wrists, point your fingertips downward, and lift your elbows into the over-the-barrel position of the crawl stroke. Turn your hands to a slightly palm-out position. Lift your chin as you pull sharply in a semicircular motion—out, back, and in—with elbows bent 90 degrees and fingertips pointing directly downward (see Figure 11.1a). Breathe as you finish the pull with elbows out and palms up under your chin (see Figure 11.1b). To recover: Drop your face back into the water, bring your elbows in to your sides, but leave your hands at chin or neck level (see Figure 11.1c). Turn your hands palm down and push them forward, just under the water, fingertips leading, into full arm extension again (see Figure 11.1d). Normally a kick and a long glide would follow, but with no kick to provide propulsion your glide will be very short. Exhale on the glide.

The pull should feel as if you were digging your fingertips into the water ahead and using them to pull your body through between them. Your elbows must remain as high as you can keep them until they are pulled in to your sides. Propulsion should come from the palm of your hand, first pulling outward and back and then inward and back to your chin. The entire pull is completed forward of your shoulders, and your hands should never pull past shoulder level. Each hand moves approximately in a small half-circle from full extension to your chin.

FIGURE
11.1

KEYS TO SUCCESS

BREASTSTROKE ARM PULL
Execution

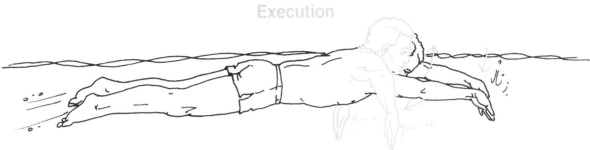

a

1. Wrists flex; fingertips drop ___
2. Elbows lift; palms turn out ___
3. Elbows bend 90 degrees; fingertips point down ___

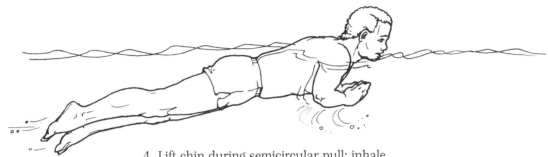

b

4. Lift chin during semicircular pull; inhale ___

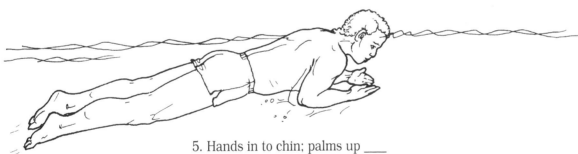

c

5. Hands in to chin; palms up ___
6. Elbows in; face down ___

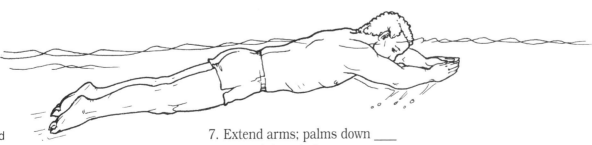

d

7. Extend arms; palms down ___
8. Long glide; exhale ___

The Breaststroke

The breaststroke coordinates the breaststroke kick, which you learned in its inverted position as the elementary backstroke kick, and the breaststroke arm pull. Converting the elementary backstroke kick into the breaststroke kick should not be difficult. The only difference is that you now "drop" your heels *up* instead of down behind you. Pull and inhale while you recover your legs to "cocked" position, kick as your arms shoot forward into glide position, glide and exhale.

Why Is the Breaststroke Important?

This stroke requires very little energy because your arms recover under water and natural flotation keeps you afloat. When swimming long distances, this low-energy stroke becomes a lifesaving factor. You have learned that you can rest by turning over onto your back to keep your face free of the water. In choppy waves sometimes the back position is not the most comfortable. The breaststroke offers an alternative and permits you to see where you are going at the same time. This stroke provides the easiest method for keeping your head above water while in a prone position.

How to Swim the Breaststroke

From a prone-float position (see Figure 11.2a), start the breaststroke arm pull and head lift. While pulling and lifting your head, bring both heels up behind you in the breaststroke kick recovery (see Figure 11.2b). Inhale quickly, and as your hands rotate during the elbow squeeze, your feet should be rotating outward in preparation for the leg thrust (see Figure 11.2c). Drop your face down into the water as you thrust your hands forward and kick vigorously. Streamline your body and take a long glide as you exhale (see Figure 11.2d).

FIGURE
11.2

KEYS TO SUCCESS

BREASTSTROKE

Preparation

a

1. Prone glide ___

BREASTSTROKE
Execution

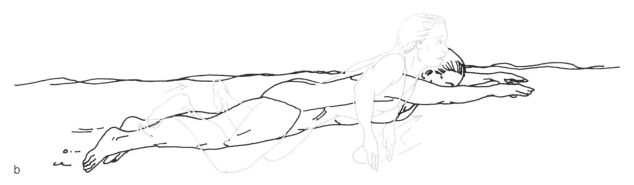

b

2. Pull, raise head, heels up ___
3. Feet hooked, turned out ___

c

4. Hands under chin; feet move out ___
5. Head drops; legs thrust; arms extend ___

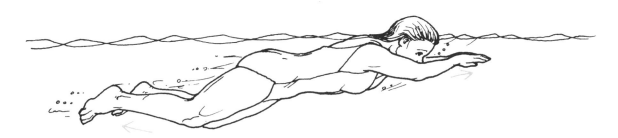

d

6. Long glide; exhale ___

More rules govern the exact movements for the competitive breaststroke than for any other stroke. An error in the arm, head, or foot position can disqualify a swimmer. Some of the common errors committed by novice swimmers are listed below. Use the suggested corrections to eliminate the errors.

ERROR / CORRECTION

Breaststroke Pull

ERROR	CORRECTION
1. Your pull is too wide.	1. Bend the elbows 90 degrees as your pull moves outward; point hands down, not out.
2. Your elbows drop too soon.	2. Reach over the barrel to pull.
3. You pull too far back.	3. Keep your elbows forward until your hands reach your chin.
4. Your breathing is wrong.	4. Lift your chin forward at the beginning of the pull; inhale at the end of the pull; put your face down for the glide and exhale.

Breaststroke Coordination

ERROR	CORRECTION
1. Coordination is lost.	1. Think "pull, kick, glide," not "kick, pull, glide."
2. Your head and body rise.	2. Do not *lift* your head, just thrust your chin *forward* to the surface. Do not press *down* with your hands, pull *back* instead; elbows high.
3. Your head goes under water.	3. Keep your hands at the surface on the glide; chin up.
4. One foot turns in and engages the water with the top of the foot.	4. Illegal kick; hook your ankle and turn both toes outward.

DRILLS

1. Slow-Motion Breaststroke Pulls

In shallow water attach the deep-float leg support to one ankle. Put on your mask and snorkel. This will allow you to concentrate more on the arm stroke without worrying about breathing.

Start from a prone float with your arms extended. Flex your wrists, point your fingertips downward, and lift your elbows into the over-the-barrel position of the crawl stroke. Turn your hands to a slightly palm-out position. Tilt your chin to look straight forward as you pull slowly in a semicircular motion—out, back, and in—with elbows bent 90 degrees and fingertips pointing directly downward. Inhale as you finish the pull with elbows out and palms up under your chin.

To recover, bring your elbows in to your sides, but leave your hands at chin or neck level. Turn your hands palm down. Push them forward, just under the water, fingertips leading, into full arm extension again. Exhale. Do not raise your head. Move your arms in very slow motion without thought of propulsion. Concentrate on correct arm and hand positions as you float (review Figure 11.1).

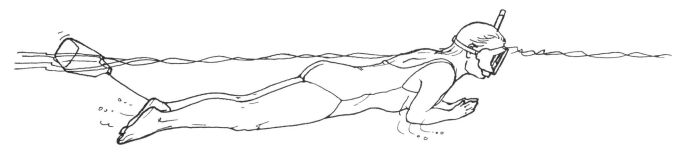

Success Goal = 20 correctly executed slow-motion arm strokes ___

Success Check

- Even though you have a snorkel, inhale near the end of your pull and exhale in glide position ___
- Go slowly through the motions while floating ___
- Concentrate on arm and hand positions ___

To Increase Difficulty

- Gradually increase the speed of the pull until you are getting some forward movement.
- Breathe in correct coordination.

To Decrease Difficulty

- Use a "pull-buoy"-type float.
- Breathe at will, not in correct coordination.

2. One-Arm Breaststroke Pulls

Hold a kickboard in one hand and wear a deep-leg support float, your mask, and snorkel. Float face down. (Do not raise your head during this exercise.) Move one arm through the breast-stroke arm-pull pattern in slow motion. Emphasize the high-elbow position. The forearm and hand should move in a semicircle, hanging down from a high, bent elbow. Keep your palm facing the direction of motion as it circles.

Shift the kickboard to the other hand and work with the opposite arm.

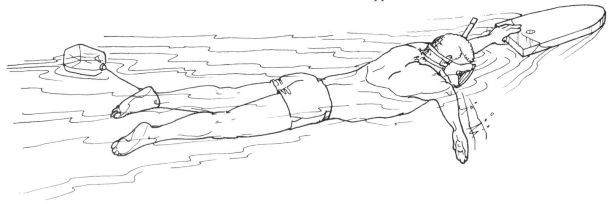

Success Goal = 30 practice pulls with
each arm ___

Success Check
• Simply float, do not try for propulsion ___
• Concentrate on hand and arm positions ___
• Drill each arm separately ___

To Increase Difficulty
• Eliminate the kickboard.
• Breathe in correct coordination.

To Decrease Difficulty
• Use a pull-buoy-type leg float.
• Breathe at will, not in correct coordination.

3. Breaststroke Pulls for Propulsion

Use the leg support float, but eliminate the mask and snorkel. Change the emphasis on practice pulls to gain propulsion. Dig in forcefully with your fingertips and thrust your chin forward; pull sharply and quickly with the forearms and hands to the position under your chin and inhale. Bring your elbows in, drop your face into the water, and thrust your hands forward easily. Stop and glide. Exhale. Try again.

Success Goal = 40 quick, hard pulls with
coordinated breathing ___

Success Check
• Pull hard; recover easily ___
• Inhale at the end of the pull ___
• Exhale on the glide ___
• Do not raise your head; thrust your chin forward ___

To Increase Difficulty
• Lift your heels behind you as you pull; thrust with both feet together as you extend into your glide.
• Eliminate the leg float.

To Decrease Difficulty
• Use a pull-buoy-type leg float.
• Use a float belt.
• Use a mask and snorkel, but thrust your chin forward and breathe in proper coordination.

4. Breaststroke Pull With Leg Thrusts

Use a pull-buoy-type leg float held between your thighs. Keep your feet together. As you pull with your arms, bend your knees to lift your heels behind you. Then, as you extend your arms forward, kick downward sharply with both feet. Inhale on the pull; exhale on the glide. Keep the pull short and quick and thrust your arms forward with the leg thrust. Do not pull your hands past your shoulders.

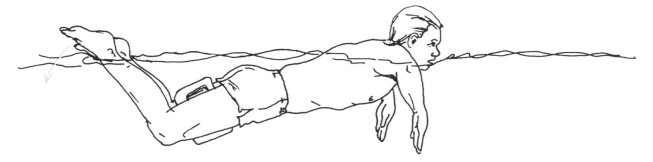

Success Goal = 1 pool width or 15 yards ___

Success Check
- Raise your heels as you pull; feet together ___
- Pull hard and breathe ___
- With relaxed ankles kick backward with feet together as you thrust your hands forward and drop your face into the water ___

To Increase Difficulty
- Eliminate the leg float.
- Hook your ankles and turn your toes out, but keep your feet together.

To Decrease Difficulty
- Glide, float, and rest as you think about the next stroke.
- Wear a mask and snorkel to allow yourself to concentrate on the pull.

5. Breaststroke Pull With Breathing

Repeat Drill 4, but start by exhaling before the first pull. Then, using the pull of your hands to help, lift your chin forward until it is at water level. Open your mouth and inhale as your hands pull inward to your chin. At the end of the pull, while your elbows are squeezing inward, drop your face back into the water. Thrust your arms forward; exhale on the glide. Be ready to lift your chin again on the next pull. Be careful not to press down on the water more than is absolutely necessary to thrust your chin forward. Keeping your elbows high helps keep the pull in the right direction.

Success Goal = 20 consecutive pulls with successful breathing ___

Success Check
- Chin forward to water level ___
- Inhale as hands pull inward ___
- Drop face in, exhale on glide ___

To Increase Difficulty
- Pull one pool width.
- Keep your chin forward.

To Decrease Difficulty
- Wear a mask and snorkel.
- Glide longer.

Review the breaststroke kick in the elementary backstroke position. Then turn over and grasp the top of the pool edge or overflow trough with one hand. Position the other hand directly below, palm against the wall and fingers pointing to the bottom of the pool. By pulling on the top hand and pushing with the lower hand (gently), you can hold a position with your feet near the surface. If your body swings to one side, move the bottom hand slightly toward that side. When comfortable in the bracket position, bring both heels up behind you in the breaststroke kick recovery. Allow your legs to sink far enough to keep the heels under water. The kick is identical to the elementary backstroke kick. Avoid bringing your knees under you. Keep your thighs in line with your body.

Practice the breaststroke kick in the bracket position, concentrating on the backward thrust with the inside of your ankle.

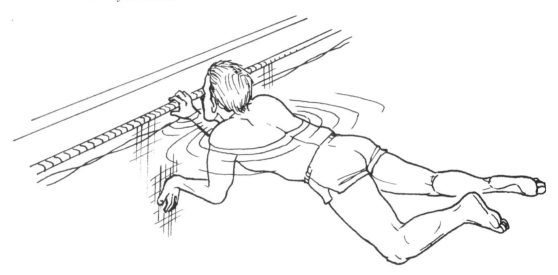

Success Goal = Feel the thrust of your feet driving you against the wall ___

Success Check
- In bracket position keep your thighs in line with your body ___
- Raise your heels; hook your ankles ___
- Turn your toes outward ___
- Kick out, around, back, and squeeze ___
- Point your toes at the end of the kick ___

To Increase Difficulty
- Keep both hands in front of you, but don't grasp the pool edge. Keep your face down as you kick; scull and raise your head for a breath between kicks.

To Decrease Difficulty
- Wear a mask and snorkel; keep your face in the water as you practice.
- Wear a mask and snorkel; keep both hands on the top of the pool edge, don't press downward.

7. Breaststroke Kick Against Resistance

Repeat Drill 6 with someone standing behind you and placing their hands on the inside of your ankle. Their fingers curl up over the soles of your feet as you kick against their hands. *CAUTION! DO NOT PUSH VERY HARD. THESE ARE WEAK MUSCLES.*

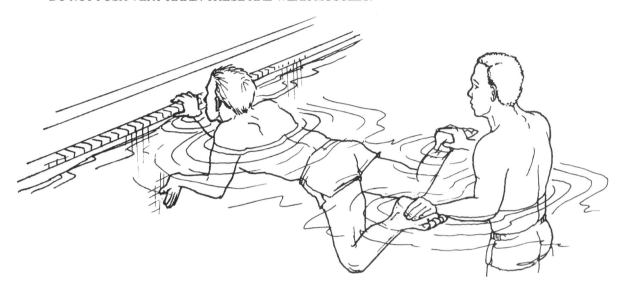

Success Goal = Feel the pressure when you kick ___

Success Check
• Do not bring your knees down under you ___
• Allow your legs to sink far enough to keep your heels under water ___
• Feel the pressure of the inside of your foot and ankle against your helper's hands ___

To Increase Difficulty
• Turn away from the pool wall. Push yourself forward through the water against the resistance of your helper's hands. Keep your face in the water while kicking and raise your head to breathe between kicks.

To Decrease Difficulty
• Wear a mask and snorkel and keep your face down.
• Keep both hands on the pool edge.

8. Breaststroke Kick With Kickboard

Hold a kickboard at arm's length with both hands and practice the breaststroke kick for propulsion. Keep your chin as low as possible to breathe. Do not bring your knees in under your body on the recovery. Bring your heels up behind you. Your hips should bend only very slightly.

Success Goal = 1 pool width or 15 yards ___

Success Check
- Thrust your chin forward to inhale as your legs recover ___
- Drop your face into the water and exhale on the glide ___
- Hook your ankles, turn your toes out, and drive with the inside of your feet and ankles ___
- Streamline and glide ___

To Increase Difficulty
- Discard the kickboard and scull with your hands while inhaling.
- Increase the distance to 30 yards.

To Decrease Difficulty
- Wear a mask and snorkel and keep your face down, but inhale on the recovery and exhale on the glide.
- Put your arms on top of the kickboard and grasp the front end of the board with your fingers.

9. Breaststroke Coordination With Mask and Snorkel

Float on the surface, face down, with mask and snorkel. With absolutely no thought about propulsion, work on the coordination between arms and legs. Start lifting your heels as the pull begins. Hook your feet and point your toes outward as the pull finishes. Move your feet outward while your elbows squeeze in to your side. Thrust out, around, and back with your legs as your arms extend forward, palm down.

Do this drill in *very slow motion* while floating.

Success Goal = 40 slow-motion strokes ___

Success Check
- Pull and inhale while your legs recover ___
- Kick while your arms thrust forward ___
- Glide; exhale ___

To Increase Difficulty
- Gradually add propulsive power after 10 strokes.
- Try for one body-length glide.

To Decrease Difficulty
- Wear a float belt.
- Take only 25 slow-motion strokes.

10. Breaststroke Coordination (no Aids)

Begin with a stretched prone float. Exhale and begin to raise your head on the first stroke. Pull for propulsion and inhale during the stroke. Drop your face back into the water as your hands come in under your chin. Exhale after the leg thrust as you glide in stretched position. Do one stroke at a time and ride your glide while you concentrate on the beginning movements of the next stroke (see Figure 11.2, p. 121).

Success Goal = 20 strokes with coordinated breathing ___

Success Check
• Exhale in float position ___
• Raise your chin and inhale during the pull, while your legs recover ___
• Drop your head and kick as your arms move forward for a glide and exhalation ___

To Increase Difficulty
• Pull and kick with power; try for one body-length glide.
• Continue for 50 yards.

To Decrease Difficulty
• Wear a float belt.
• Pull just hard enough to lift your chin.

11. Breaststroke—Distance per Stroke

Swim the breaststroke with emphasis on the length of the glide. Try to cross the pool in two or three strokes by pulling and thrusting with power and stretching the glide.

Success Goal = 3 yards per stroke average ___

Success Check
• Take a big breath on the pull and hold it ___
• Kick into your glide and hold your breath until your forward motion stops; exhale ___
• Take another breath on the next pull and repeat the procedure ___

To Increase Difficulty
• Count your strokes across the pool. Decrease the number by one.

To Decrease Difficulty
• Wear a float belt.
• Exhale, inhale, exhale after your glide and before the next stroke; inhale on the pull.

With a lifeguard watching you, start at the deep end of the pool. Push off in a prone glide and swim a fully coordinated breaststroke to the shallow end of the pool or 25 yards.

Success Goal = 15 yards or more in deep water ___

Success Check
- Push off and exhale during the glide ___
- Pull, inhale, and recover your legs ___
- Kick, thrust your arms forward, glide, exhale ___

To Increase Difficulty
- Push off the *side* of the deep end; swim and turn toward shallow water.
- Swim to the shallow end; turn and swim back to the deep end.

To Decrease Difficulty
- Wear a float belt.
- Swim slowly; concentrate on coordination.

With a lifeguard watching you, start at the shallow end of the pool. Swim breaststroke to the deep end of the pool. Grasp the edge of the pool, tuck your legs, and pivot. Place your feet against the wall and push off. Hold your glide for 3 seconds before beginning the breaststroke. Swim to the shallow end and repeat the wall turn. Continue swimming for 100 yards.

Success Goal = 100 yards ___

Success Check
- Maintain a steady, even rhythm with a long glide ___
- Exhale during your glide off each end wall ___

To Increase Difficulty
- Eliminate your glide; have someone time you for 100 yards.
- Swim and glide easily for 200 yards.

To Decrease Difficulty
- Wear a float belt.
- Rest before turning at each end wall.
- Have a friend swim with you.

14. Breaststroke Adaptation

Swim the breaststroke with your head above water and chin at water level constantly. Allow your feet and legs to drop into a semivertical position; do not try to glide at all. Constantly alternate leg kicks and arm strokes to maintain your position, but don't try to rise above chin level. Breathe whenever you wish. Make forward progress slowly. This "conversational" adaptation of the breaststroke is one of its nicest features.

Success Goal = 5 minutes of easy head-up swimming ___

Success Check
• Swim slowly and easily ___
• Keep your face clear of the water ___
• Stop your kick just short of full extension ___
• Start another arm stroke just before full extension of your arms ___

To Increase Difficulty
• Use wide sculling motions instead of the breaststroke arm pull.

To Decrease Difficulty
• Wear a float belt.
• Breathe at will.

ELEMENTARY BREASTSTROKE SUCCESS SUMMARY

One advantage of the breaststroke is its adaptability for swimming with your head always above the water. That form of the stroke is not its defined form, however. Ask a breaststroke expert or swimming coach to examine your stroke to make sure you are swimming it within the narrow definitions established by the competitive swimming rule books (see Figure 11.1 and Figure 11.2).

STEP
12 DIVING: FALL IN GRACEFULLY

Entering the water is easy: Simply go to the edge and fall in. Just how you fall in is the subject under consideration in this step. You can jump feet first, fall in flat, or dive gracefully. You can even use a springboard to propel you into the air like the all-time great diver Greg Louganis, but you cannot call yourself an accomplished swimmer until you can do a fully coordinated standing front dive.

CAUTION! WATER DEPTH IS CRITICAL FOR ALL DIVING SKILLS! YOU MUST HAVE A WATER DEPTH OF 10 FEET FOR SAFETY IN THIS STEP. Failure to have adequate water depth can result in serious injury, including concussion, broken neck, and quadriplegia.

Kneeling Dive

In adequate water depth, this kneeling dive is both safe and easy to learn. It is the first step in learning an easy, standing dive.

Why Is the Kneeling Dive Important?

The kneeling dive teaches you how to enter the water smoothly, how to emerge from a dive, and how to do a shallow dive to avoid injury. Don't skip this important step!

How to Do a Kneeling Dive

Assuming your site has a deck height of 12 inches or less *and* adequate water depth, stand at the edge of the pool and hook the toes of one foot over the edge. Kneel on the opposite knee. Stretch your arms overhead, intertwine your thumbs, and squeeze your arms against your ears. It is important to keep your ears buried between your arms. Bend over until your hands are slanting down toward the water (see Figure 12.1a). Rock forward, take a breath and hold it, keep your chin down, and push off with your toes. Lift the rear leg. Push *out* into the water (see Figure 12.1b). Hold your breath, arch slightly, point your hands and head upward, and rise to the surface.

FIGURE 12.1 KEYS TO SUCCESS

KNEELING DIVE

Preparation

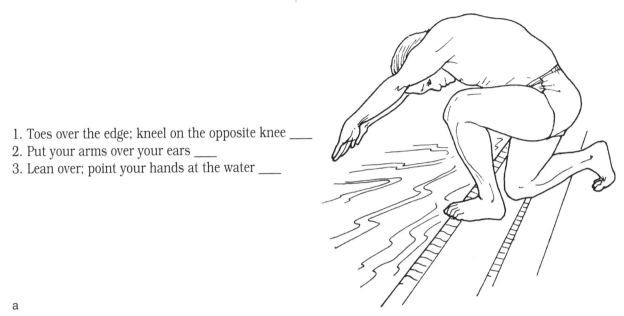

1. Toes over the edge; kneel on the opposite knee ___
2. Put your arms over your ears ___
3. Lean over; point your hands at the water ___

a

Execution

b

4. Take a deep breath; chin down ___
5. Rock forward; push off ___
6. Lift your rear leg; dive out ___
7. Arch; turn your head and hands up ___
8. Glide to the surface ___
9. Exhale; swim to the edge ___

One Foot Dive

CAUTION! THIS DIVE REQUIRES A WATER DEPTH OF AT LEAST 10 FEET.

You have learned to do a kneeling dive that carries you out at a shallow angle. Expert divers try to enter the water vertically. A stretched, vertical entry with very little splash is the mark of a good dive. Adequate water depth is required for safety because a vertical entry carries you deeper.

Why is a One Foot Dive Important?

The 1-foot dive is a transition from a low-position, shallow dive to a stand-up dive that can be used from nearly any height. This dive can be learned from the deck to gain confidence and then taken to the low diving board for a new experience.

It is important because it helps eliminate painful flat dives that result from skipping progressive steps.

How to Do a One Foot Dive

AT A DEPTH OF 10 FEET OR MORE, stand with one foot forward, one back. Grip the edge with the toes of your forward foot. Extend both arms overhead covering your ears. Hook your thumbs and squeeze. Bend forward. Aim at a point only 3 feet from the edge (see Figure 12.2a). Point the toe of your rear foot. Lift your rear leg high over your head as you rock forward into the water. KEEP YOUR FORWARD KNEE LOCKED STRAIGHT to keep you a safe distance from the pool wall. Enter the water vertically. Keep your hands over your head for protection (see Figure 12.2b). When submerged, tuck your knees and turn back to the surface. Pull downward with both arms to aid you in surfacing.

**FIGURE
12.2**   KEYS TO SUCCESS

ONE-FOOT DIVE
Preparation

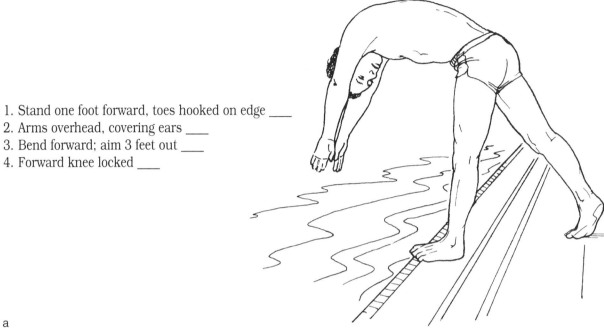

1. Stand one foot forward, toes hooked on edge ___
2. Arms overhead, covering ears ___
3. Bend forward; aim 3 feet out ___
4. Forward knee locked ___

a

Execution

5. Point rear-foot toes; rock forward ___
6. Chin down; LOCK FRONT KNEE ___
7. Rear leg high; vertical entry ___
8. Tuck ___
9. Turn toward surface ___

b

Standing Front Dive

CAUTION! LEARN THIS DIVE IN A MINIMUM WATER DEPTH OF 10 FEET.

A standing front dive is one of the basic skills in personal water technique. It is a means for entering the water, but it also is a tell-tale mark of an accomplished swimmer. It allows you to enter the water with grace, charm, and precision. It is as much esthetic as utilitarian.

Why Is a Standing Front Dive Important?

Diving is a sport separate from swimming, but closely related to it. The standing front dive is the elementary technique in a whole series of more complex skills. It is not important to swimming, per se, but is a skill expected of, and desired by, nearly all swimmers. It is important in that it may open an entirely new area of sport interest for you. Try it. You'll like it.

How to Do a Standing Front Dive

Be sure you have at least 10 feet of water depth and no underwater obstructions. Stand with the toes of both feet gripping the pool edge, arms at your side. Swing both arms in a small circle (12 inches in diameter): out, back, around, and forward past your hips (see Figure 12.3a). As your arms circle, bend your knees slightly. As your arms pass your hips, spring upward. Bend fully at the waist, lifting your hips behind you (see Figure 12.3b). Continue the arm swing until your hands point 4 feet out from the edge. Tuck your head between your arms and lift both legs behind you, straight and stretched. Enter the water vertically (see Figure 12.3c). Tuck your knees; or arch and turn your head and arms up to glide to the surface.

FIGURE 12.3

STANDING FRONT DIVE

1. Toes grip edge; hands at side ___
2. Circle arms; bend knees ___

a

Execution

3. Spring upward; lift hips ___
4. Aim 4 feet out; bend double ___
5. Chin down; lift legs ___

b

c

6. Body straight; vertical entry ___
7. Arch; lift head and arms; glide ___

DIVING SUCCESS STOPPERS

Diving requires a completely different kind of coordination and timing than swimming. It involves new movement techniques and kinesthetic senses. Errors in timing and body position can sometimes result in painful water entries. You can avoid many of the common errors by using the correction tips presented here.

ERROR	CORRECTION
Kneeling Dive	
1. You are hitting flat.	1. Tuck your chin; keep your ears between your arms; lift your trailing leg higher.
2. You are diving too deeply.	2. Look farther forward; lift your head; bend your wrists back to point your fingers up.
3. Your glide is too short.	3. Keep both legs straight; stretch and streamline.
One-Foot Dive	
1. You are hitting flat.	1. Stay bent at the hips; keep your chin tucked in; raise your rear leg higher.
2. Your rear foot strikes the edge of the pool.	2. Keep your front knee locked; lift your rear leg higher.
3. You do a complete somersault into the water.	3. Lift your chin a little; allow your hips to straighten as you enter the water; bend your wrists back on entry.
4. You make a big splash.	4. Point your toes; keep your legs stretched until they are under water.
5. Your body crumbles into the water.	5. Be brave; have faith; try again.
Standing Front Dive	
1. You are hitting flat.	1. Think somersault—a dive is 1/2 a somersault. Tuck your chin; get your hips up behind you; lift your legs; get more spring.
2. You are hitting too far out.	2. Jump up, not out. Imagine you are diving over a low fence; think about jumping into a handstand on the water 3 feet out. Aim for the bottom.
3. Your legs are apart.	3. Squeeze!
4. Your knees are bent.	4. Stretch!
5. Your toes are not pointed.	5. Whose toes are they?
6. You make a big splash.	6. Hold a streamlined position to the bottom.
7. Your legs go over too far.	7. Keep your body stiff and stretched; raise your chin; look at the water.

DRILLS

1. Underwater Glide

In chest-deep water with your back against the wall, stretch your arms overhead to cover your ears. Put one foot against the wall behind you, take a deep breath, put your face down, aim your hands slightly downward to dig in to the water, and push off. Streamline and glide underwater as far as you can.

Success Goal = 10 underwater glides ___

Success Check
- Keep your arms over your ears ___
- Hold a deep breath ___
- Aim down hill ___
- Streamline and stretch for your glide ___
- Glide until you stop or need a breath ___

To Increase Difficulty
- Start while floating with *both* feet against the wall in tuck position.
- Stay as close to the bottom as you can for as long as you can.

To Decrease Difficulty
- Wear goggles so you can see under water.
- Glide for a count of three, then raise your chin and turn your hands up.

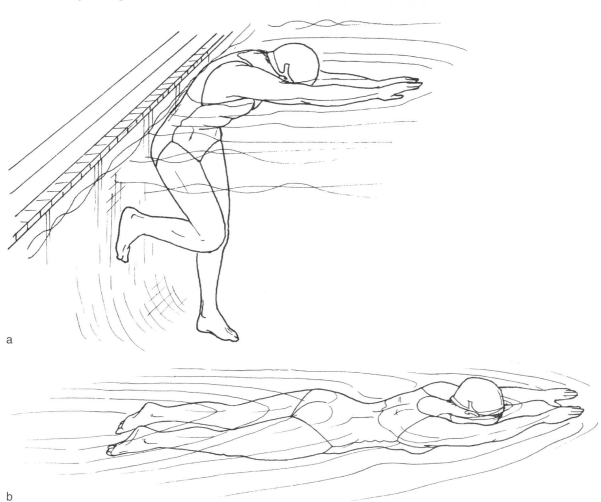

a

b

2. Glide Through The Hoop

Get a hula hoop that floats. Tie a small weight to it so it sinks, but stands on edge on the bottom. Set it about 8 feet from the wall in 5-foot depth. Standing with your back to the wall, stretch your arms overhead covering your ears, interlock your thumbs, and squeeze your arms tight to your ears. Take a big breath, put your face in the water, and tuck both legs. In face-down, tucked position, place both feet against the wall, aim downhill toward the hoop, and push off. Glide through the hoop; turn your hands and head up to rise. (The hoop distance may be adjusted.)

Success Goal = 10 successful passes through the hoop ____

Success Check
• Keep your arms over your ears ____
• Face down, lift one foot against the wall behind you, then the other foot; push off ____
• Aim for the hoop; hold your breath ____
• Stretch; streamline your body; glide ____

To Increase Difficulty
• Move the hoop farther away.
• If your glide slows too soon, kick to maintain forward movement.

To Decrease Difficulty
• Wear goggles so you can see under water.
• Move the hoop closer.

3. Kneeling Dive

Move to an area where the water depth is 10 feet or more. Stand at the edge of the pool; hook the toes of one foot over the edge. Kneel on the opposite knee. Stretch your arms overhead, intertwine your thumbs, and squeeze your arms against your ears. It is important to keep your ears buried between your arms. Bend over until your hands are slanting down toward the water. Rock forward, take a breath and hold it, keep your chin down, and push off with your toes. Lift the rear leg. Push *out* into the water. Hold your breath, arch slightly, point your hands and head upwards, and rise to the surface (review Figure 12.1, p. 133).

Success Goal = 10 kneeling dives in good form ___

Success Check
- Hook your toes firmly over the edge ___
- Keep your arms squeezed tightly over your ears ___
- Bend over; point your hands slightly downward ___
- Push off; straighten and raise the trailing leg ___
- Glide; turn upward to the surface ___

To Increase Difficulty
- Dive deeper; see if you can touch the bottom.
- Hold your breath and extend your glide.
- Try to slip into the water with no splash.

To Decrease Difficulty
- Do *not* wear goggles; they will come off.
- Have a friend in the water to guide your entry.

In water 10 feet deep, do one kneeling dive; then prepare for a second kneeling dive. This time, before you push off put all your weight on your forward foot and the toes of your rear foot. Raise your knee about 6 inches (15 cm) off the deck so you are in a "track-start" position. Dive. Repeat with the knee a little higher.

a

b

Success Goal = 5 track-start dives, each one with your knee a little higher than the last ___

Success Check
• Keep your arms pressed tightly over your ears ___
• Aim downward toward the water ___
• Raise your knee off the deck ___
• Dive, straighten, and lift your rear leg high ___

To Increase Difficulty
• Start with your rear leg straight.
• Stretch both legs together on the entry.

To Decrease Difficulty
• Have someone in the water to direct your hands.
• Have someone on deck lift your leg.
• Don't look at the water; look at your toes.

5. Correct One-Foot Dive

AT A DEPTH OF TEN FEET OR MORE, stand with one foot forward, one back. Grip the edge with the toes of your forward foot. Extend both arms overhead and cover your ears. Hook your thumbs and squeeze. Bend forward. Aim at a point only 3 feet from the edge. Point the toes of your rear foot. Lift your rear leg high over your head as you rock forward into the water. KEEP YOUR FORWARD KNEE LOCKED STRAIGHT to keep you a safe distance from the pool wall. Enter the water vertically. Keep your hands over your head for protection. When submerged, tuck your knees and turn back to the surface (review Figure 12.2, p. 135).

Success Goal = 10 one-foot dives with
vertical entry, straight legs, pointed toes, and no splash ___

Success Check
- Keep your chin down ___
- Stretch the rear leg and point your toes ___
- Keep your forward knee locked ___
- Bend; aim in close ___
- Fall; kick the rear leg way up overhead ___

To Increase Difficulty
- Point the toes of your forward leg as it leaves the deck; stretch and point both legs.
- Carry your vertical entry down to the bottom.

To Decrease Difficulty
- Have someone on the deck hold and lift your rear leg.
- Have someone in the water touch your forward knee to remind you to keep it locked.

6. Low Board One-Foot Dive

Hook the toes of one foot over the end of the one-meter diving board. Don't bounce the board. Bend forward and lift your chin so you are looking just over your fingertips at a point about 4 feet from the end of the board. Keep your forward knee rigid. Fall forward and lift your rear leg high.

Success Goal = 5 one-foot dives in good
form from the one-meter board ___

Success Check
- One foot forward, toes over the edge ___
- Squeeze your arms against your chin ___
- Look at your fingertips ___
- Aim 4 feet from the end of the board ___
- Fall; lift the rear leg high ___

To Increase Difficulty
- Start the board rocking very gently and fall on the upward motion.
- Tuck your chin in just before water entry.

To Decrease Difficulty
- Have someone stand on the board with you to lift your leg as you fall.
- Concentrate on keeping both knees locked straight.

This drill may be performed from any low elevation, but it works best from a 12-inch height.

With water 10 feet or more in depth, stand with both feet at the edge of the pool. Grip the edge firmly with the toes of both feet. Extend both arms overhead to cover your ears. Hook your thumbs together. Squeeze your arms against your ears. Bend over until your hands point to the water about 3 feet from the edge. Do not allow your knees to bend at any time during the dive. Bend your wrists back slightly. Fall forward into the water. When submerged, lift your chin, turn your arms and hands upward, arch your back, and glide outward and upward.

Pull toward the top if you wish to hurry the ascent.

Success Goal = 3 fall-in dives or until the dive is comfortable ___

Success Check
• Hook your toes over the edge firmly ___
• Keep your arms tightly pressed against your ears ___
• Bend double at the hips ___
• Keep both knees locked straight ___
• Fall forward; allow your hips to straighten ___
• Enter, arch, look upward, surface ___

To Increase Difficulty
• As you fall, lift your legs and point your toes.
• Streamline your body and glide to the bottom.

To Decrease Difficulty
• Have someone kneeling beside you touch your knees to remind you to lock them straight.
• Have someone in the water to guide your arms.

8. Arms Down, Standing Dive

Start as for Drill 7, but leave your hands at your sides. As you bend over and start your fall, bring your hands forward into the dive position.

Success Goal = 3 arms-down dives or until comfortable ___

Success Check
- Stand with feet together and toes hooked over the edge ___
- As you bend forward, bring your arms forward to cover your ears ___
- Continue your bend and arm movement right into a forward dive ___
- Stretch your legs and point your toes ___

To Increase Difficulty
- Keep your feet together, toes pointed.
- Carry the streamlined position all the way to the bottom.

To Decrease Difficulty
- Stand with your arms well behind you to start; then bring them forward as you bend.

9. Standing Dive With Spring

Start as in Drill 8, but bend your knees slightly before starting to fall. Keep them bent until you are falling and are *definitely off balance*; then spring upward with your legs and hips and lift them behind you. You will straighten your legs in the process of jumping, so keep them straight for the entry.

Success Goal = 3 standing "fall-and-spring" dives ___

Success Check
- Bend your knees slightly, for a small jump ___
- Bend and bring your arms forward as you fall ___
- Don't jump until you are *definitely falling* ___
- Jump upward, not outward ___
- Lift your legs; point your toes; keep your chin down ___

To Increase Difficulty
- Keep your feet together, toes pointed, knees stretched for a splashless entry.
- Stay close and lift your legs to stay vertical.

To Decrease Difficulty
- To prevent jumping prematurely, have someone yell "jump" at the proper moment.

Stand erect at the edge of the pool, toes gripping the edge. Do *not* dive, but practice swinging your arms in a small circle: out, back, inward, and forward past your legs a few times. Swing them in a 1-foot circle. Each time they swing backward, bend your knees slightly; and as your hands come forward past your legs, straighten your knees as if you were jumping.

After several practice swings, think about your fall-and-spring dives. Imagine bending over and falling *as* you swing your arms forward and springing directly into a handstand on top of the water. Imagine it a few times, then DO IT! Remember, you must be falling *before* you spring.

Success Goal = 5 arm-swing spring dives ___

Success Check
- Practice swinging your arms in circles: outward, backward, inward, and forward ___
- Bend your knees slightly on the backward motion, then bend over and straighten them on the forward motion ___
- Think about falling forward and springing upward as you bend over ___
- Go ahead! Do an arm-swing dive with spring ___

To Increase Difficulty
- Repeat the dive until you can do it with a vertical, stretched, toes-pointed entry.

To Decrease Difficulty
- Do land drill arm swings and practice jumps until you are confident.
- When you feel confident, don't hesitate, DO IT!

Be sure you have at least 10 feet of water depth and no underwater obstructions. Stand with the toes of both feet gripping the pool edge and arms at your side. Swing both arms in a small circle (1 foot in diameter): out, back, around, and forward past your hips. As your arms circle, bend your knees slightly. As your arms pass your hips, spring upward. Bend fully at the waist, lifting your hips behind you. Continue the arm swing until your hands point 4 feet out from the edge. Tuck your head between your arms; lift both legs behind you, straight and stretched. Enter the water vertically. Tuck your knees or arch and turn your head and arms up to glide to the surface (see Figure 12.3).

Success Goal = 10 fully coordinated standing front dives ___

Success Check
- Stand erect; toes grip the pool edge ___
- Swing your arms out and back while you assume a slight crouch position ___
- Swing your arms inward and forward as you lean and fall forward ___
- Spring; lift your hips upward; tuck your chin ___
- Lift your legs behind you for a vertical stretched entry; point toes ___
- Tuck and turn or arch upward to the surface ___

To Increase Difficulty
- Keep working toward vertical, streamlined, no-splash dives.
- Move to a higher take-off height.

To Decrease Difficulty
- Study the standing front dive success stoppers.
- Ask a diving coach to watch you and correct your mistakes.
- Practice, practice, practice.

12. Hula-Hoop-for-Height Dive

Stand in a hula hoop ready for a standing front dive. Have someone hold the hoop at about shin or knee height, so that the hoop is about 1 foot in front of your legs. (Have it held from the side so the holder won't get kicked with your heels.) Dive up and over the hoop, being careful to get your head down for a *vertical* entry. Keep your entries close to the wall (within 4 feet).

Raise the hoop a little each dive to see how high you can dive to clear it.

Success Goal = 10 standing hoop dives at knee height ___

Success Check
• Use a large arm swing; lift your arms in front ___
• Spring *up*, then bend and lift your hips ___
• Lift your legs and point your toes ___
• Tuck your chin and stretch for entry ___

To Increase Difficulty
• Move the hoop higher (thigh high).
• Swing your arms higher to aid your lift.
• It takes many dives to achieve high, vertical, splashless entries.

To Decrease Difficulty
• Keep the hoop low.
• Use a stick instead of a hoop to dive over.

13. Fully Coordinated Standing Front Dive From the 1-Meter Springboard

Stand on the end of the 1-meter diving board with your toes over the edge. Practice some arm circles for a standing front dive. Notice that as you practice arm circles, the board bounces. Get your arm circles in rhythm with the board's bounce so the board is rising as your arms move forward and upward (see Figure a). Select an upward arm lift and board bounce to launch your dive. Use the upward movement of the board to give your dive more height (see Figure b). Keep your chin up a little more; the board will lift your legs (see Figure c).

a

b

c

Success Goal = 10 standing board dives with a streamlined vertical entry ___

Success Check
- Hook your toes over the end of the board ___
- Let the board set the rhythm; match your arm circles to the board rhythm ___
- Select an upward motion to lift your takeoff ___
- Dive *up*, then bend and raise your hips and legs ___
- Chin up; watch the water; tuck your chin for entry ___

To Increase Difficulty
- Back up two steps. Take a step and a hop. Land on the board with both feet with your toes about 1 inch from the end. Time your arm swing to be moving down and forward as you land on the board. Lift with your arms and spring upward into a high forward dive. Keep your entry close, vertical, and streamlined.

To Decrease Difficulty
- Do a standing front dive on the first bounce.
- Keep your whole body stiff for the entry.

DIVING SUCCESS SUMMARY

Diving requires precise timing, a finely honed kinesthetic sense, and hours of practice. Consider the fact that the time of each dive is only 5 seconds from start to entry, and you can see why so much practice is necessary. You cannot do a dive in slow motion to study the proper moves. It moves at its own speed. For this reason it is best to work with an experienced diving coach if you aspire to proficiency. Modern video tape technology enables divers and coaches to study each dive in slow motion. Use Figures 12.1, 12.2, and 12.3 to guide you in learning. If you have mastered the techniques in this text, you are ready to move on to advanced swimming skills and refinements.

RATING YOUR PROGRESS

Congratulations! You have worked through the 12 steps to success in swimming. Perhaps the greatest success goal you can achieve is to feel comfortable in the water and confident in your ability to handle water emergencies.

The second "success goal" in a swimming course is your actual swimming progress. How many strokes and how many dives did you learn? How well did you learn them? Are you pleased with your progress?

Successful Swimming Inventory

The following self-rating inventory should lead you to some interesting conclusions. Read the questions thoughtfully and answer them with care. Then reflect a bit on the profile that emerges. What were your strong points? your weak points? Do you care enough to put more time and effort into strengthening those weak points? What are your swimming goals?

Psychological Phase:

To what degree have you overcome your fear of the water?

___ Totally ___ Some ___ None

___ Still maintain a healthy respect

Do you think you could save yourself if you were to fall into the water?

___ I could ___ Don't know ___ Never

Have you gained significant confidence?

___ Yes ___ No

Do you enjoy the water?

___ Much ___ Some ___ Not at all

Did you have fun learning?

___ Lots ___ Some ___ None

Physical Phase:

Which of the following skills did you learn? How well did you learn them?

	Very well	Well	O.K.	Poorly
Back float	____	____	____	____
Sculling	____	____	____	____
Back support kick	____	____	____	____
Back crawl kick	____	____	____	____
Basic back arm pull	____	____	____	____
Basic prone stroke	____	____	____	____
Turning over	____	____	____	____
Sidestroke	____	____	____	____
Crawl stroke	____	____	____	____
Elementary backstroke	____	____	____	____
Breaststroke	____	____	____	____
Front dive	____	____	____	____

Overall Swimming Progress

Considering all the psychological and physical factors you marked above, how do you rate yourself?

____ Very Successful ____ Successful ____ Unsuccessful

Do you want to continue learning advanced swimming skills?

____ Yes ____ Many ____ A few ____ No

ABOUT THE AUTHOR

David G. Thomas has been a swimming teacher and coach since 1948, when he became a water-safety field representative for the American Red Cross. In 1955 he became swimming coach and director of aquatics at Berea High School, Berea, Ohio. Eight years later he moved to the State University of New York at Binghamton, where he was director of aquatics and swimming coach until retiring as Professor Emeritus in 1985.

Thomas gained nationwide prominence in 1972 by producing a textbook, teaching guide, exams, and visual aids for training swimming pool operators. The *Swimming Pool Operators Handbook* and the other materials were published by the National Swimming Pool Institute as the basis for its Certified Pool Operators program.

Since retirement, Thomas has focused much of his attention on writing. He has published many articles on aquatic subjects and is a contributing author to several books on swimming pool design and operation, including *Professional Aquatic Management*. He is the author of *Teaching Swimming: Steps to Success, Advanced Swimming: Steps to Success, Competitive Swimming Management*, and the *Water Is Friendly: The First Step in Learning to Swim* video.

A consultant in aquatics and pool design and operation, Thomas lives with his wife, Virginia, in Anderson, SC. He enjoys scuba diving and boating in his leisure time and swims a mile each day for fitness.

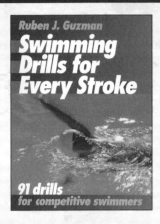
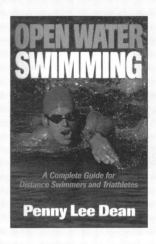

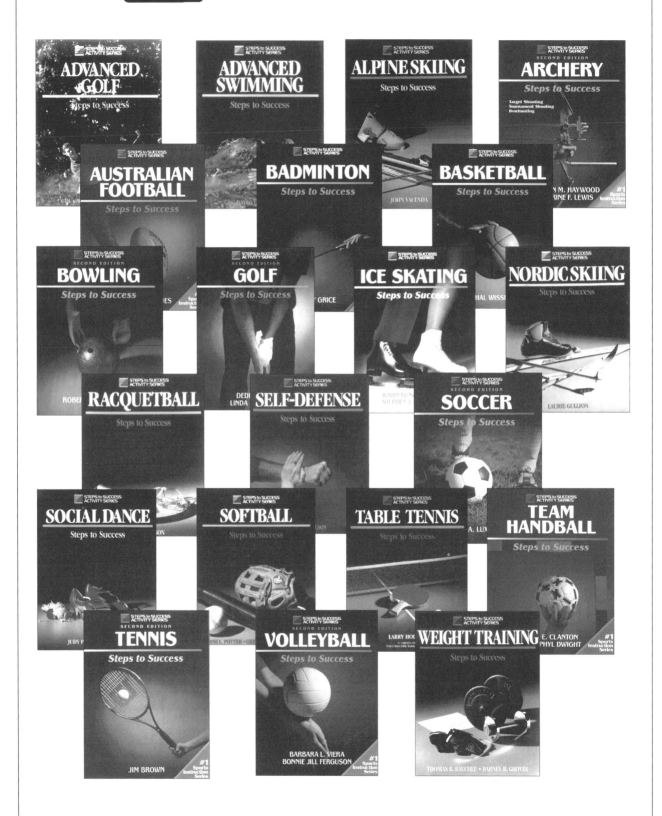

Other books in the
Steps to Success Activity Series

Instructor Guides also available. Contact Human Kinetics TOLL-FREE for prices.